Letters to Betty

The Anatomy of One Woman's Grief

Mary Bub

GREEN HEART
LIVING
— PRESS —

ISBN Paperback: 978-1-954493-82-7

Published by Green Heart Living Press

Cover photography by Mary Bub

Cover design by Elizabeth B. Hill

Grief box illustrations by Anna Harteau

Photography and paintings by Mary Bub

DEDICATION

As a young woman just beginning my journey into the world of helping others to find their own sense of self, their authentic voice, I was blessed by an invitation to join a small group of like-minded women who called themselves Bethany. The reference to Bethany came from the scriptures that tell the story of two women, Mary and Martha. Through a circle process, Bethany met with women for extended weekends to explore issues of self-care—emotional, physical, and spiritual.

This book is dedicated to the women of Bethany. They challenged my creative bone and nurtured me on my own journey as a writer, artist, poet, and facilitator. They taught me the true meaning of process. My time with my Bethany sisters taught me lessons that have sustained me throughout my striving to invite women to find their authentic voice.

MARY BUB

Sometimes grace falls

From the sky

Like summer rain.

It fills the soul

With a nurturing presence

One can only feel

Grateful

Mary M. Bub

CONTENTS

Foreword   1

Introduction   3

September   11

October   15

November   39

December   73

January   107

February   147

March   187

April   227

Glossary   235

Acknowledgments   237

About the Author   239

FOREWORD

When I initially met Mary, I had no idea how my life would change. But change it did. In her, I met my match in the feisty independence and self-doubt categories. Her confidence is infectious. She is a wonderful amalgamation of empathy, sympathy, support, and tough love with an amazing ability to see and interpret the needs of those around her—friend or not. This quiet, immensely talented, adorable, emotionally intelligent woman alternately raises my consciousness and then blows my socks off with her insight into behaviors of self and others.

She will listen intently with a slight sideways cock of the head, gauging intent, analyzing outcomes, and then will proceed to adroitly delve into and expertly take aim at the heart of an issue. And she's spot on, delivering a realistic, caring, supportive, and calming influence to those in the throes of emotional stress. You can be assured that when Mary delves into an emotional question she will pop out the other side with an analysis delivered in decisive calm.

I read *Letters to Betty* alternating between sobbing, nodding in agreement, reliving past experiences, and looking back lovingly at lost loved ones. The journey detailed in these letters is one we will all take. How we navigate is up to the individual, but who doesn't love and appreciate having a road map close to our destination? Loss and death do not have to be crippling or frightening. But they often are. As we walk with Mary through her journey of honest assessment, we learn by example how to address those emotions we think we should feel and those we don't want to admit. We are encouraged to thoughtfully explore a confrontation with our own longing. Longing for the world to never change from that one perfect, happy moment that, hopefully, each of us may experience in our lives.

Lis Friemoth

Entrepreneur, artist, community activist, friend

INTRODUCTION

For better or for worse, for richer or poorer, in sickness and in health, until death do us part. This is the promise that I made to my partner on my wedding day. I can say that we accomplished all of the above conditions.

No one wakes up one day and says, "I can't wait until I am into the grief, mourning, or bereavement process." Here in the middle of my own process, I realize that we are in this process during the whole of our lives. Being born into life in itself suggests that we have entered a journey. Born into something, the beginning of something, we soon come to learn that the something is our life story. We experience the life cycle of nature, we are confronted early on by the movement of the sun and the moon, from day to night, too painfully we experience the death of members of our families, our friends, our community. And we grieve.

How might we walk through this end-of-life process openly, authentically, and with grace? I really didn't know. I have always used letter writing as a way to process the events of my life. Two things were important for me: sharing my thoughts and emotions truthfully and writing as though I was talking to someone who I trusted to listen. It came to be Betty, an imaginary person that I borrowed from a song lyric.

When I found Betty, the writing began. I was aided in this process by the use of symbols and metaphors. One of them I call the grief box. It became a key character in the telling of my story. You will soon find metaphors that helped me describe my feelings on any given day. I hope that you find some of your own; they are helpful when words just don't come.

The grief process is at times a long, difficult process and at others a blessing. I hope to share through these writings my own personal journey. The hard parts, the grace-filled parts.

Grief is like a roundabout. There are many paths and if you miss your exit, you just keep going around and around. Finally, one day you take the exit and then the journey truly begins.

I was a come-late-in-life child. My sisters were 11 and 13 years older than me. Therefore, my relatives were also much older than I was. Some of my most vivid memories are attending funerals for family members, friends, and neighbors. As I grew into adulthood, helping to arrange these events became part of my responsibility. I remember well a time when my dad, who is long gone now, took me aside and told me that I had done a good job. Although there are many other things I would have been happy to hear from him, I took it as high praise.

In my work as President, facilitator, and Gathering Circle leader of a small non-profit, I am proud to say that through my 25-year tenure I sat in circles with more than 2,200 women. Most of them were farm and rural women. In these circles, I heard many stories of loss. It is in these Gathering Circles that I developed a deep respect for the value of story. The writing of them, the sharing of them, and the lasting effect that they have on the listener when shared in a safe place with no judgment.

One day I chose to exit the roundabout. I knew that I had to find a way, a process, that would help me on my personal journey of grief. Many of my friends have moved to other parts of the country and so communication in letter form has become our way to stay in touch. Perhaps this was the way. I began writing to my alter ego who I named Betty. Each day I sat in front of my keyboard and waited for the words to tell Betty what I was feeling or thinking or doing that day. The book that you have in your hands now is the result of my letters to Betty.

It is my deep and sincere hope that by sharing my story and my letters to Betty you will know that you are not alone in your loss, there are many kinds of loss, and there is no one-size-fits-all process for healing a grief-stricken heart. There is grace to be found if you, too, decide to take the exit off of the roundabout. There is a process that is just right waiting for you.

Grief never ends, but it changes.

It's a passage, not a place to stay.

Grief is not a sign of weakness, nor a lack of faith ...

It is the price of love.

Elizabeth I

Ordinary Things

It was five days after Don died. I was at the dentist getting a permanent filling to replace the temporary one after a root canal. Of course, being a gentle and compassionate man, the dentist noticed that I was not myself. I told him about Don and he told me about his wife. She had died within the year as well. What he shared with me has stayed with me and given me practice for each and every day. He said, "Every day just do one ordinary thing. You will continue doing all of the extraordinary things but that one ordinary thing will help you to stay grounded. It will give you purpose and meaning."

I have found his words to ring true. Each day I wake and decide what my one ordinary thing will be for that day. As time goes on, I find myself doing more than just one ordinary thing. Perhaps this is how one finds their way on this very unpredictable journey that we call grief.

SEPTEMBER

September 15, 2023

Dear Betty,

The grief box is an imaginary box that resides in my head. It is a safe place and in it are stored all of the emotions and maybe even some thoughts about my grief and its journey. The grief box almost fell off the shelf today. When this happens, everything comes spilling out. It is usually not a great day when this happens. Instead, I started to think about which pieces I did not need any longer. Just where am I in the process everyone calls "grief"? Still sad and lonely, I find myself feeling remarkably grateful. I think my fractured pieces are starting to be put back together.

Memories, wonderful, needed, and fickle. I heard myself talking to Lis, the friend that I don't want to share with anyone else. She listens to me, questions me, supports me and together we work through deeper questions than 'What do you think about climate change?' But as usual, I digress. What I noticed was I talked about Don and I didn't get emotional or even the least bit weepy. I actually felt proud about the way he responded to a situation that he felt was unfair. He acted out of his values and was willing to take the consequences.

Back to memories; for days I couldn't let myself go to the place of any memory without crying. So, pulling out the stoic part of me I just stopped trying to remember anything. Wisdom: It is far better to remember and cry than to deny oneself the contents of learning that can be had from each and every memory. Isn't it how we are supposed to keep our loved ones with us? Aren't they supposed to reside somewhere in our soul or in the marrow of our bones?

Memories can be wonderful. We need them. We can choose to allow them to be fickle or instead a source of deep comfort. Especially when they are shared.

Soon,

Me

OCTOBER

October 3, 2023

Dear Betty,

When will I stop feeling fractured? I know it will take a while. So, I have been told by many people. This doesn't mean that I have to like it.

Barb Murray, the woman who will be officiating Don's Celebration of Life, called this morning. She is not feeling well and so we have moved our meeting to next week to talk about it. I cannot say that I am sad about this. Hopefully I will be in a better place by then. Not so exhausted all of the time and not weeping every two minutes over nothing.

It is a bright, shiny day, 80 degrees with a little breeze. Not bad for October. Not looking forward to winter.

Till next time,

Me

October 9, 2023

Dear Betty,

It is another Monday and it is hard to believe that Don has been gone more than a month already. Days seem long now that all of the busy work is finished. It keeps you going for a while. When all of the notifications, thank you notes, and cards stop arriving you begin to understand that life goes on. One cannot stop the clock from counting the seconds and minutes and hours. Still, I want to rewind it to a time when Don was truly present and not only resting in my mind and heart.

It is true that memories are golden and I have been blessed with 60 years of them. What is 60 years in the grand scope of the universe? It seems at times as though it was just a drop in a pool of glistening water. The ripples are far-reaching to our family, friends and all of the experiences that we had the grace and blessing to share.

Thank you so much for your kind words and prayers. You are often in my thoughts. I am sending you all good and peace. Be well and happy in yourselves and care for one another always.

Wishing for a rewind,

Me

October 10, 2023

Dear Betty,

Feeling lost, lonely, and sad. I know that this is part of the process and that I will find my way again. I miss Don, and he would say, "Ya... like a toothache." He would be wrong. It is the ache of a fractured/broken heart. I am sure that we have nicked one another's hearts from time to time, but we never caused a wound that felt like this. He is always on my mind and in my heart.

Bye,

Me

October 15, 2023

Dear Betty,

Reached into the grief box today and picked out sadness and loneliness. I am beginning to recognize myself in a state of sadness. It is not as painful as anguish. It is just in me, dulling my voice and my vision. Not to the point of darkness but rather more like a thin veil that moves in the gentle wind allowing for brief moments of light.

I have experienced loneliness in a crowd but this kind of loneliness is quiet, maybe a little moody, but not strong enough to make me want to reach out and ask for company. It is more like the absence of a presence that should always just be there. It is like a fine painting that has hung in the same place for years and years until one day someone decides to remove the dust behind it. It cannot be replaced but the outline remains longing for what once was.

Bye for now,

Me

October 16, 2023

Dear Betty,

Went to Strumpet & Tart yesterday. Always good to sit with Lis for conversation. She is a special person and really helps me process things. I only fear that it is too much about me and I have to make an effort to engage her in things that she is doing/experiencing as well.

I am going to spend some time in the studio today, going to the bank and the post office. Joan and Wayne, such good friends, have invited me to go with them to the flower domes in Milwaukee tomorrow. I said yes reluctantly but I did say yes.

Caryn, my oldest daughter, left today for her herding club experience in Minnesota. I hope she has a good time and that it will be a good break for her. Like all of us, she is missing her dad and their frequent conversations. For a quiet hermit, Don's presence looms large for all of us. The grief box may be in place for some time. Maybe forever.

All for now,

Me

October 20, 2023

Dear Betty,

Cloudy today, fall is in the air. It makes me feel a little moody. I am not accomplishing much of anything today. Thought I would be doing a lot of writing, painting and maybe even baking. Not happening.

While I had York, my faithful dog, out this morning, I had some time to listen to the birds in the bird apartment, the big evergreen trees in front of the house. We named them the bird apartment because we watched the birds go in and out building their nests in the shelter of huge soft branches. At times we would just sit and listen to their loud chattering, imagining what they must have been talking about with their neighbors. Today it sent me into a reflective mood and so today this practice found me thinking that I don't like the word "grief." On further reflection I realize that it is not the word that I don't like, it is the grieving process that I don't like. After searching for words to replace "grief" I came to the conclusion that there are no pleasant words for this process.

Perhaps this is my moving into the prescribed stage two of denial. If I convince myself that I don't like the word then I don't have to walk the path that it places me on each day and even into some nights. Not wanting to accept that I might be facing someone else's definition of grief. In my own rejection of the accepted process of the five stages of grief, I might just lose out on the understanding that they offer. Why do I think that it has to be Kubler-Ross's way, or any of the others who have prescribed or written about the stages of grief, or the highway? Why can't I accept that each way, theirs and mine, has benefits?

Well, Betty, methinks that a good helping of humility might be on my menu for today. What do you think?

Humble pie,

Me

October 22, 2023

Dear Betty,

After my missive of yesterday, I spent an amount of time thinking about how I feel and think about the stages of grief. I came across an article. Actually, I came across many articles on the subject, but I will only share quotes from the following one.

"Time to bury the 'five stages of grief' myth" - By Susan Perry | MinnPost

"Vaughan Bell, a psychologist at King's College London, notes in a recent article in the Observer that research shows 'we all grieve in our own way.'

The idea that we go through five stages of grief—denial, anger, bargaining, depression, and acceptance— when we experience a major loss, particularly the death of someone we loved, has become deeply embedded in our culture. 'Contrary to our long-held assumptions, there are no rules to grief, no stages except our personal journeys and no task except those we set ourselves,' he adds. Normality is not what we return to; it is what we go through.'"

Finding this article was so affirming for me, Betty. From the day the hospice chaplain asked Don and me if we were angry or if we felt guilty, I have stuck to my guns and talked. Rather than a stage, I might be talking about my process, my own grief journey.

I confess to you that I decided to take each of the stages as prescribed by Ross and try to relate it to my own process. Now I find myself thinking that this would be a waste of time because I would be trying to fit into a square hole when my experience is a round peg.

Today I opened the grief box and took out sadness and the melancholy of being alone on a beautiful, colorful autumn day. I don't know if I will ever be able to let sadness blow away on a soft light breeze but I confess that being pensive has proved to be helpful in bringing understanding to small bits of this journey.

Holding on,

Me

October 23, 2023

Dear Betty,

Being authentic is at best comforting and at worst heart-breaking when embarking on the grief process. This became most apparent to me two weeks after Don died.

Death is shocking. Whether you have been on a long-term journey towards goodbye or if it is sudden. I had the privilege of being with Don through all of the seasons of his illness. Although we both knew that his illness would only get worse, we also had the assurance that we were doing our best to be there for one another.

I am sure now that even though I felt that I was prepared, I was indeed in shock. I also know that I experienced anticipatory grief and guilt. During the last three months of Don's life, I found myself thinking about what life without him would be like. What or who would I have to take care of? I had been his caring person for so long. Then the sinking feeling of guilt came knocking at my door. I felt guilty about thinking about him being gone while in fact he was still there with me.

I didn't realize that I was in shock until I was sharing my feelings with a friend. In telling her that I was fatigued, I felt like I was living in some strange kind of fog, having little or no desire to eat and was certainly not sleeping well. On the other hand, I was so efficient. She told me that I was in shock. I was, and it was good of her to help me understand this part of the process.

It is what I do though, isn't it Betty? Taking care of business, making arrangements, being in charge are all of the safe places I go when it is too painful to be authentic, truthful, or trusting of myself or those around me. Getting back to my opening statement today, being authentic is comforting when I can finally step back and come home to the deep waters of who I aspire to be. It is heartbreaking when it is who I want to be but find myself isolating from those I know love me and care about me. How silly is this since I am also craving the storytelling and sharing of memories that ensure Don's presence is always with us.

Bye for now, Betty,

Me

October 24, 2023

Dear Betty,

Doing an ordinary thing each day has been helpful in setting on the path of putting one foot in front of the other. Today I realize that I am finding both grief or sadness and grace in the ordinary things. It is an ordinary thing to leave the house to go to the post office or the bank. These are ordinary things that I found refuge in, more than I needed to get out of the house for a minute or two. Now they are just another part of being alone, doing the things that Don would have done and that I gradually started to do.

No matter if I was gone for a long while or even just a little while the returning was always a welcoming home. Upon my leaving, he would say, "Drive safely, have fun" and upon returning he would say "Missed you" or "How did it go?" I find comfort in this memory because it reminds me that he cared about me and my comings and goings. There is, I am afraid, grief, too. There is no voice welcoming me home. I fear that as time goes on, I will not remember the sound of his welcoming.

Off to my ordinary thing, the post office,

Me

October 25, 2023

Dear Betty,

My pick out of the grief box today was courage. I had to go to the hospital to have my labs done for my doctor appointment next Monday. It reminded me of all of the times that I took Don there for his labs. Another sad moment, or rather, several sad moments. It also reminded me of how I watched him change. From his leaving home and saying "I am going to get my labs done, be back soon," to the time when he wasn't driving anymore. Dropping him off at the door and waiting in the parking lot, then picking him up again. The last time we performed this ritual the kind volunteer met him as we drove up and helped him out of the car. He also took him down the long corridors to the lab and waited to bring him back. What a kind man he was, always remembering Don and offering him his kind presence.

I came home and put my courage back in the box. My new thought today is this: I have found myself seeking out kind memories instead of recent ones. Yes, there is kindness in the recent memories but they are also filled with fear, sadness, loneliness, and pain. I let myself go there when I want to convince myself that I did all that I could, that I made good decisions and mostly when I want to remember the quiet times we spent together having little chats. I find that I am not dwelling on those recent memories as often. When I start to feel melancholy, I take myself to the kind memories, the happy memories and mostly the memories that take me to our time together just holding hands.

For now,

Me

October 26, 2023

Dear Betty,

While I was looking out of my office window, I was again marveling at the unique way nature has of moving us from fall to winter. There I saw the small crab apple tree that still had most of its beautiful orange leaves. But, there on the grass I saw a smattering of her fallen leaves. They were scattered not far from her in a pattern that reminded me of someone scattering seeds in the early spring.

This little tree offered me a picture metaphor for my imaginary grief box. Some of its contents scattered but so much is still holding on. I also see that some of the leaves have been blown out into the yard. Perhaps these are the bits that will soon fly away and not have to be put back into the box. Perhaps they have served their purpose and are free to move on.

Betty, I am becoming more and more aware that the grief box holds more than sadness, loneliness, and all of the other emotions that one encounters in the process. There is also awareness and gratitude and calm when I am willing to open myself to acknowledge this.

Each day I take another step on the path of discovering who I am and where I am going. And, each day you help me to see and to feel and to continue on.

Till tomorrow,

Me

October 27, 2023

Dear Betty,

It seems that I find myself spending an amount of time wondering. Today's wondering brought me to the question, "When did I change from partner to caregiver?" In the literal sense, I suppose it was when we first received the first diagnosis. But in retrospect, I have come to believe that I have always been a caring person. I cared for Don when we married, I cared for our children when they were born, I care for our grandchildren and great-grandchildren. I care.

The journey changes dramatically when the shift happens from caring to caregiving. Caring is an emotional response to loving, to wanting the best for another person. Caregiving demands a hands and heads choice to doing tasks that take time and an inner resource that you didn't even know that you had. It may not always allow for the time or space you need to be your authentic self. Still, I do believe that I did my best to be an authentic caregiver and partner.

So, the answer to my question turns out to be: I have always both cared and given care to Don.

I am grateful that we were able to maintain our partnership making decisions together but realizing that I was always caring, caregiver and partner.

Till then,

Me

October 28, 2023

Dear Betty,

There was nothing ordinary about today. I went to the bank to close our joint account. I went to another bank to take his name off of an account and to get a credit card in my name only. Then, I went to the Department of Transportation to have the title for the car changed from his name to mine.

It was a long day and not one I would have chosen. Each time I have to do these extraordinary things I have to explain why. I have to repeat over and over again, "My husband died."

I returned home both emotionally and physically tired.

All for now,

Me

October 29, 2023

Dear Betty,

Gray and cold today. I guess that could describe how I feel. Gray, not black or white, a bit colorless. It is Sunday and I am finding that weekends are not my favorite time of the week now.

Went grocery shopping today and did not get carried away. I am not feeling creative in the cooking arena. Had eggs and toast for lunch and will probably have something equally simple for dinner.

I still find it hard to come back to the house after doing errands like grocery shopping or going to the post office. It is facing the quiet and the emptiness each time, waiting for the familiar "Is that you? How did it go?"

I will proceed to doing my one ordinary thing now; vacuuming makes me feel as though I have accomplished something, a good distraction.

Soon,

Me

October 30, 2023

Dear Betty,

Even though the sun is shining and the fall trees are still showing their colors all along the treeline, I find myself feeling gloomy. I don't feel very well today. Have a little sore throat and little energy.

Something tells me that I should identify my feeling today as lonely. I could settle for that but I just don't find that completely accurate. I want to find a way to express this feeling of "missing." I think I have to find more noise in my life. When there is solitude and easy quiet, I find myself continually missing. I miss Don's presence, his just being here. Sure, I miss his voice and our morning rituals. I even miss his way of procrastinating until I made the decision about whatever it was that we were trying to decide. Mostly I miss holding his hand.

Would making my life noisy really help me feel less empty, less missing? I know the answer and I will just keep on keeping on this sorting of the questions in my grief box.

Until again,

Me

October 31, 2023

Dear Betty,

Had lunch with a friend today. Really didn't want to go because it was cloudy and snowy and I didn't have a good night. However, I did go and now am glad that I did. It seems that I need to take these opportunities to step out for a minute into the reality of life around me. It would be too easy to just hunker down with my woes and let the world go on but that has never been the nature of my being.

Happy Halloween! I think I will let the rest of this day be my treat. I will cozy up in my chair and let myself drift off into a nap. Tomorrow will be a new day and I will find an ordinary thing to do, maybe laundry.

Be well,

Me

NOVEMBER

November 1, 2023

Dear Betty,

Ordinary things today: banking and laundry. I am feeling like the days are too long and I need to start doing things other than ordinary things. But, what?

I don't have much or any incentive to paint or write or get involved with others.

It would just be too easy to sit in my chair and watch TV. That doesn't work either, though, because I just get bored and antsy.

I am going on a long weekend to enjoy the fall season. Maybe getting away will give me a boost or at least get me out of my 'poor me' funk.

Let you know when I return,

Me

November 5, 2023

Dear Betty,

It was good to get away for a bit. Good to be in another environment. Riding through the countryside this time of year is always a treat. Most of the color has been erased from the landscape but it is replaced with a very luscious rust brown. It is pretty dramatic against the yellow gold of the corn still on the fields.

I felt an old energy that I haven't felt in some time. Not an "oh boy, let's get going" kind of energy but a calm and quiet pleasure at doing something not ordinary.

I recognize that even in the calm enjoyment of the moment there is an empty space in me that I foresee will never be filled up in the same way again. It is that still small voice that says, "He would have loved this, or look at that, isn't that interesting?" Again, I can still hear his voice but fear that it too may be quieted at some time. I struggle to know what to keep in the grief box and what to let go of. I want to always hear his voice but I wouldn't mind letting go of the sadness inside when I feel that it will fade. I will try to smile when I remember familiar phrases that were always so just him.

So long,

Me

November 7, 2023

Dear Betty,

Alone. I have come to think that what I am experiencing now is a new kind of alone. At least it is a different kind of alone for me. There is the kind of alone that I have always known as a quiet way of being on my own. I have at times longed for time alone. There is the kind of alone that can be isolating or the kind that means only you alone have the answer. Today I am feeling alone in my grief journey. As hard as others may try to understand, to be empathetic, or to relate my aloneness to their own story, only I can really know this kind of alone.

I guess that is it. I am not sure that I understand this kind of aloneness. It is different than feeling alone in a crowd because when I feel that, it is either because I don't feel like I belong, or I am simply not interested or maybe understood.

My alone feeling today includes knowing that others somewhere are having the same feeling and I expect that only they can understand it. Each of us travels this journey exclusive of anyone or anything else and so our alone feeling is ours to own. We can empathize, sympathize, share our feelings, and try to understand, but in the end, I will add it

to the grief box and accept that it is mine and it is
OK.

Tomorrow,

Me

November 8, 2023

Dear Betty,

Not feeling like I have much to say today. Feeling sad and noticing that the changing season is slowly creeping up on me. Cold and damp today. I am turning on lights to create a warmer and more comforting atmosphere.

One grace of the day came when I was reading something on the Universal Life Church website. At the very bottom of the article, I found the words "Go placidly amid the noise and haste, and remember what peace there may be in silence."

Don't you think that this is a grace, Betty? It is from the "Desiderata", one of the readings from Don's memorial service. It was one of his favorites, not just that one phrase but the whole reading. Just as I am sitting here alone in the quiet and wondering how I got here and where I may be going next, this one particular phrase pops up on my screen as though it is meant just for me today.

I have to ask myself, "What is the noise in my life today and why am I in such a hurry to make haste?" Perhaps the noise is the ringing in my head like a bell that won't stop saying, "Grief is this and that and you are experiencing this and that, and above all it takes time."

Never being one to follow the conventions of the day, I rebel and say, "Not me, you are talking about someone else." Still, I admit that I am at one stage or another. Yes, I am sad, and yes, I am lonely, and yes, I at times feel purposeless but lots of others feel these things as well. Why must we always give things qualifiers? Why must we list things and call them stages or number the lists? A difficult place for a rebel to find herself in, yes Betty? I will do my best to remember the second part of the phrase, remember what peace there may be in silence. Be still my monkey mind!

I guess that I did have something to say today. And I am going to try to find grace in every day. Today it was as though he was reminding me of the words that he did truly try to live by. They are grace and I am grateful.

So long Betty,

Me

November 9, 2023

Dear Betty,

Last night I went out for a social evening. It was the first time that I joined a group of peers in a while. It is a comfortable and fun group of folks to spend time with, some of them married and some of them not.

I found myself remembering cliches like, "Two is company, three is a crowd" or "like a wallflower" or "on the outside looking in." Everyone in the group knew why I hadn't been there for the past several months but still no one said anything about it. I felt like the elephant in the room. It was during another part of conversation that I saw one of the folks lean over and whisper to the person sitting next to her, "She just lost her husband."

I would like to think that especially as an older person I would be able to be direct about death and grief. This is truly a learning experience. I vow to be open about my journey if in fact anyone is brave enough to ask me about it.

In our world we have come to expect clear, concrete answers to our sadness or out of control feelings. I have come to understand that this is not how feelings work. We really don't want to hear the sentimental words found in sympathy cards even though we know that the sender meant so well.

I have heard that there are no two snowflakes alike. I have no scientific evidence of it myself. I have never tried to compare them. I take it on faith. So too I have come to understand that no one else has or will ever experience grief in the same way that I am.

My challenge is to be willing to share the magnitude of my grieving without feeling embarrassed or inadequate or ashamed that I cannot control the process. As I write this, Betty, I realize that I have just told you what a control freak I am. Something is askew in my imaginary perfect world. So much for being authentic.

Till then,

Me

November 11, 2023

Dear Betty,

Today the grief box is leaking tears. It was so yesterday as well. I continue to tell myself that I am only two months into this process and that I would not have wished it for myself or anyone else for that matter. I remember what I told the chaplain when we first met, "I know the stages of grief, we will go through the process and we will come out of the other side." How bold of me to make that declaration. I have no idea where the other members of the family are in their own process or if they can even think of their grief in those terms.

Most people feel a need to tell the story, to find someone willing to hear what others cannot and who can join them in making sense of the death without withdrawing into awkward silence or offering trite and superficial advice. Storytelling and story catching are healing.

What do you make of this Betty? I found myself wondering if I want someone to bear witness to this journey. What exactly does it mean to be a witness to someone's grief without giving in to the urge to lessen it or reframe it? I really like the bit about not pointing out the silver lining because I am not sure that there is one. What is the silver lining to grief? Perhaps it is affirming to know that another person traveled life's road with me, that I loved and was loved. Can I not know that without the pain of this loss?

I do find that sharing the stories and encouraging the catching of stories that should not be forgotten is important. You will remember on an earlier date I said that memories are both wonderful and fickle. Or something like that. I had a fickle memory the other day. I remembered a doctor's visit that I attended with Don. He told the doctor about a concern that he had and the doctor replied with a non-answer and dismissed him. The memory made me just as angry in the remembering as it did when it happened ages ago.

How do I encourage the storytelling that I so want to be a part of and that I want to hear? I don't want to put a pin into another's pain but I long to know their stories because it may give me more insight into the man at the heart of my grief. So, I say goodbye, feeling sad but embracing the journey, I think.

Any answers, Betty?

Me

November 11, 2023

Dear Betty,

Yesterday I asked myself the question that I dislike when others ask it of me. "How are you?" Same old answers: "OK, fine, alright."

"What was I feeling" was a better question. The answer surprised me. I said, "I am feeling wobbly."

What does that mean? The image that came to mind was of one of those bop-it toys that kids get. It is made of rubber and is flat on the bottom, narrow on the top. You hit it and it falls over but pops back up. That is what grief feels like. When you least expect it, it overwhelms you and you fall over. The trick is to ask why and when you will get back up. Sometimes it is in a flash of a moment and at other times it may be a day or two or who knows how long. I think it is about finding your center and coming back to it again and again.

Like my grief box, I am going to hold on to this image and let myself wobble a bit. Besides I like to say wobble.

Wobble on,

Me

November 12, 2023

Dear Betty,

I went shopping yesterday. It was a bit overwhelming as there were lots of other folks out and about as well. I was taken aback by all of the Christmas decorations but thought I shouldn't be because it seems like the seasons get rushed more and more each year. I did find it a bit disconcerting. Again, I realized that I may perhaps be finding being at home a bit too comfortable. This thought took me to the place of knowing that sometime I will have to choose between this and that. Do I want to remain alone, feeling sad or doleful, or do I have to give into the part of me that wants to be out and about seeing new things, learning new things, meeting new people?

Today I am at home again, feeling safe and unhurried. I will do at least one ordinary thing at some time today but I am feeling more reflective. Can choosing reflection and quiet become a hiding place? If I am choosing who and what I want to reflect on I do not feel quite as vulnerable to what might slip out of the grief box. Reflection is different from remembering. At least for me, anything can happen when I choose memories.

Betty, maybe I am just looking for ways to control something that is uncontrollable. No road signs on the journey through grief.

All for today,

Me

November 13, 2023

Dear Betty,

This morning I found a quote about enthusiasm and it of course got me thinking about what I may or may not be enthused about. But first I want to tell you about what happened to me yesterday.

After the jarring shopping day on Saturday, it was a quiet day yesterday. I am finding that weekends seem endless. I was feeling a bit heartsick and at the same time really restless. I was puzzled by the contradictions of these feelings.

Guilt knocked on my mental door as I told myself that I was being disloyal to all that was locked away in the grief box. How could I feel so restless? Of course, I miss him every day and believe that I always will. What else am I missing that could make me feel so uneasy? My conclusion was that I do miss all of the ordinary things that I did for him, for our home, for the family and for myself. I tell myself that it has only been two months and therefore I am not allowed the permission to even give one moment of thought to moving on. Betty, I think this is not helpful and may even be foolish.

Another day and I am back to mourning. Found this quote this morning: "Years may wrinkle the skin, but to give up enthusiasm wrinkles the soul," (Samuel Ulman, poet.) What the hell does this mean now? Can we simply say I don't want to wrinkle my soul, and therefore I will be enthusiastic today? I don't think so. I wonder when was the last time that I felt enthusiastic.

One of the synonyms of enthusiastic is eager. On one hand, I am eager to feel centered, whole again, on the other I fear moving will dull my memories or the place in my heart or in my grief box where I have stored all of the goodness of our lives together.

Here are the things that I think I can say that I get enjoyment from or that I am avid about: meeting a friend for lunch, seeing the Kindreds and family, and playing with my dog. Another synonym is passionate. Not feeling very passionate about anything much on this journey. I might say that I am still caring but dolefully passionate.

Painting distracts me and, I will concede, even makes me happy. And Betty, writing to you each day has given me a discipline that I have only felt in regards to caring. You help me sort things out and you give me a platform for my discontent.

Today I will be on the lookout for a graced moment and I will try not to wrinkle my soul. Come on enthusiasm, my door is open.

Soon,

Me

November 15, 2023

Dear Betty,

Do you believe that if you put your words out into the universe or write them down on paper to send to your friend, they will somehow return to you? I have been trying to find peace in the silence and today I sat down to write to you and felt quiet. 'This can't be,' I thought, 'there are so many emotions that I am putting back into the g box.' Not today, though. Today I find myself thinking that my sitting in silence has produced peace. I am equating this quiet in my soul with peace.

I am no fool. I don't believe for a minute that this is the lasting peace that the poets write about, but for today I will embrace it. Today I am grateful for this quiet moment; it is grace.

Be well,

Me

November 16, 2023

Dear Betty,

No light and airy words for you today, Betty. The first word out of my mouth this morning was "shit." I was snuggled in my bed hoping for just a little more time to hide in my covers when the phone rang, thus "shit." It turned out to be a pleasant call and then I felt bad about cursing it or maybe the day.

Also feeling a little like a fraud today and here is why, after all of the things I told you yesterday about feeling quiet and reflective when the tides turned, the g box fell off of the shelf AGAIN. I spent several hours catching the tears that were spontaneously sliding down my cheeks.

I received a letter from the funeral home about a memorial event that they have each year to remember those who have died. It was a lovely letter. Nonetheless, my first reaction was, "I am not going." I feel the same way today.

What was it about that letter that set me off? Maybe nothing, maybe it just happens. This spontaneous grieving, I am afraid to say, has become almost normal for me. Perhaps I don't want to continue to memorialize Don or others that I don't even know. That sounds really mean and uncaring and not really what I am feeling. Moving on to life present day is my goal and so continually creating more memorials feels to me like being stuck in the same place. Like a record whose needle is stuck, the pain just keeps on repeating itself.

Weep I will, Betty, but I know that if I let myself try to remain as authentic and honest as I can, I will get through this time of my life, my process. Little by little each day I find myself thinking about him holistically. I think I would do him a disservice if I keep on holding on to the last moments of his life and do not honor and grieve all of who he was and will always be to me. Human.

Gotta go,

Me

November 17, 2023

Dear Betty,

Today I am sadder than yesterday but hopefully less sad than tomorrow. The word woebegone came to mind this morning. One of the definitions is "feeling sorry as in a sorry state of affairs."

I had a dream in the early hours of today. You know, the kind that happens after you have been up and go back to bed hoping for just a little more sleep. Anyway, I dreamt that Don and I were at a picnic. The picnic was over and I asked him to pick up the chairs. Of course, he didn't move as quickly as I wanted him to and this was so like him. I asked again and after a few minutes he did help put the chairs away.

What should I learn from this dream? I could get all Freudian but I am not a Freudian scholar. So, Betty, I wonder if the message for me is what I really want is for him to help me through this grief process darn it! Why can't he help me pick up the pieces? New question to self: ask him what he would want me to do with some of these feelings. What would he do in this situation?

I suppose I should write to you about what you think about the idea of talking to someone who has died but I have already decided that for me it is a healthy way to process my feelings. After all,

I talked to him for many, many years even if he wasn't always listening. It is a sorry state of affairs.

Must say goodbye,

Me

November 18, 2023

Dear Betty,

After more reflection about just what it is that makes me not want to engage in the world outside my door, I decided to take another look at the invitation to the memorial gathering.

Remember the other day I told you about the memorial gathering that I was invited to in December? Well, I have given it some more thought and I am still not wanting to attend. I have however come to a better understanding about why I don't want to attend. I think that I just don't want to let myself be in a situation where I am vulnerable. I mean what if something touches something in me and I start weeping in the middle of the service? Or what if someone wants to share their story with me and I don't know how to be compassionate or more truthfully, I don't want to be wrapped in their pain? So, what a nice person I am! I don't want to attend because I might be vulnerable and I am not compassionate either.

This invitation has been a grace given to me. I didn't even think twice before saying that I would not attend. Now I have a better understanding about myself and the new things residing in the g box. I have made judgments about myself and I have made judgments about the guy directing the service even though I don't know anything about him.

Why couldn't I just admit that I am afraid of what I might do or who I might meet? Maybe I am even afraid that someone else might have something to share with me. Am I turning away from the opportunity to learn something about this journey? Maybe I would even meet someone who is wise and who has a compelling story to share. The answer for me remains I am just not ready. I will try to do better in the judgment department both about making judgments about myself and others.

Judgment and vulnerability are tucked back into the grief box for now but I am glad that I had them fall out and I am glad for the lessons I am learning.

For now,

Me

November 20, 2023

Dear Betty,

I am sorry that I didn't write yesterday. I have just had two days of deep sadness and tears that flow at a time of their own choosing. I want to say that I guess that I was not successful at getting vulnerability back into the box but honestly, I was not and am not feeling particularly vulnerable. I am not sure what I am feeling.

Here is what happened. We had a small family gathering the other day. We met to talk about whether or not we would keep up the produce garden and Papa's Produce Stand. Don always grew produce. When our first grandson was born his name changed to Papa. Ever after everything that had to do with him was Papa's; Papa's produce, Papa's tractor, and well, Betty, you get the idea. It was decided to go ahead with these things for another year. No problem there.

It is what happened next that I think threw me back into the fray. The grandsons proceeded to talk about who would be responsible for cutting Nana's (my) grass. I truly appreciate their help but what I was feeling was not appreciated. I felt myself sinking into the couch as though I could make myself invisible. It was hard to listen to them talk about me and my grass as though I was no longer independent, as though just like Papa they would have to take over when he could no longer do it all. I am not Papa. I could go on and on about this but I would rather tell you about the conclusion.

My overwhelming sadness and teariness I think was about me realizing that I am not only mourning my lifelong partner and love but also my own identity. Oh, I know that I still have many hats to wear. I know that I feel much younger than my years would assess. Letting the memories about our, my, younger years out of the grief box reminds me of days gone by, challenges met, for sure many things that I will not do again. I admit that my image has changed for my family and I will try my best to embrace the one that they may need. Thus, my willingness to let myself add more thoughts and feelings to the grief box.

Betty, by now you understand how impatient I am. Thank you for being there for me to process this journey into the unknown and for helping me find some understanding.

So long for now,

Me

P.S. I am grateful and love my family and I am proud of them and the kind and considerate adults that they have become.

November 21, 2023

Dear Betty,

Cloudy today. I am realizing how often the weather seems to give me a hint about how I am feeling. I am feeling cloudy today, nondescript, wondering if this sad blank feeling will just be the underlying way of my emotional health. Today I will focus on ordinary things, like vacuuming and laundry.

Two days away from Thanksgiving. I do have plenty to be thankful for but methinks that in some way it also makes the missing more acute. It was a tear-stained weekend. So far today is better but Betty by now you realize along with me that that can change in a heartbeat.

I think I will let myself just be cloudy today. Who knows what tomorrow will bring?

That's about it,

Me

November 22, 2023

Dear Betty,

I don't even know where to begin today. Last night Roger, my son-in-law, went to his mother's apartment to check on her. He sadly found her dead. She didn't seem to be sick and had visited the doctor for her regular checkups. Of course, the whole family is once again in shock. I know that we all knew what was ahead for us with Don. We traveled the road of his illness for a long time. Still, when he died, we were in shock. How much more difficult is this for Roger?

Needless to say, I am feeling sad, disconcerted and I think even a bit frustrated. Once again, we are all asking, "What has happened, how could this happen, what should we do, and more importantly who should we be?"

I was with them last evening and for the first time in a while I felt like I had something to share. I felt empathy and I wish I could ease the pain.

Grateful for you,

Me

November 26, 2023

Dear Betty,

I know that I haven't written for the past couple of days. I put a lock on the grief box believing that it would help me through the holiday weekend. It almost worked. Now I realize that everything that I have practiced in the past, all of the things that I have shared with the women I have met, is true. You can only stuff your emotions down so far or for so long. If you are a person who is trying to live an authentic life your intent and your truth win out in the long run. The lock comes off and you just don't know what is going to spill out.

Still, I am glad that I, for a little time, felt in control. There it is again. The need to be in control, to control, to be the strong one, the one with all of the answers. I don't think that I want to be that person. Betty, is there good control? Yeah, I am sure there is and I believe that we all need to exercise it for our own good and the good of others. I am not talking about controlling others or every situation in my life. Rather I am talking about controlling my emotions, my words, my behaviors.

You know, there is a time for everything, a time to cry and a time to laugh, a time to grieve and a time to dance.

As I leave the grief box open, will I learn what to control and what to leave to time?

Soon,

Me

November 29, 2023

Dear Betty,

I have been helping Christy and Roger, my daughter and son-in-law, with the funeral arrangements for his mom. In some ways, it brings back memories of the not-so-long-ago things I was doing to prepare for Don's memorial. I will confess to you, however, that it has been good for me to focus on someone else and to be busy focusing on the memorial service.

I have been trying to find a metaphor for the sadness I feel now. It seems like it is easier to talk about what is not than what it is. This sadness is always just there. It rests somewhere deep inside me, not consuming me but just resting there. This morning I thought it might be like a cloak that surrounds me and rests on my shoulders. That seems like it would be too easy to throw off so I am back to searching for the right words or images. Maybe I will never be able to name it. What I know for sure is that it is not ever going to go away. It is now part of my being, my essence, my soul.

Bye,

Me

November 29, 2023

Dear Betty,

My question today is "What happens when griefs collide?" I feel that I am juggling all of the sad and lonely, challenging, and doubtful issues that come with grief. I really do believe that I will never stop grieving Don. But maybe now I am slowly beginning to realize that there are things that I may be grieving that I will not hold onto forever. Of course, there are health issues, retirement issues, family issues, or rather, relationships that are on a continuum of ebb and flow, change and staying the same.

Given that our family is experiencing yet again the loss of an elder, it is only reasonable that there would be another round of grieving.

Does one overshadow the other? Does one distract me from the process that I have already begun?

I will admit to you, Betty, that these past days of being a helper and a planner and a support person have actually given me a different sense of who and where I am. I have been feeling useful. I have also been feeling a little guilty. Then I remember the card that my dear friend sent me that tells me, "It will be over when it is over."

I will add, "It will simply be part of the story of a fine relationship."

Be well and happy,

Me

November 30, 2023

Dear Betty,

The Christmas tree is in the stand and fully decorated. It is a lovely little tree and I am glad that I decided to have one this year. I am beginning to see or maybe feel how this first holiday season without him is going to be. I anticipated a lot of tears and sadness at Thanksgiving and now while decorating the tree. I am happy to tell you that although that veil of sadness that I have told you about remains settled into my very being it was not overwhelming and the grief box didn't spring open.

Unpacking all of the old ornaments was just as reminiscent as ever but unpacking the memories of all of the year's past was pleasant and only a little melancholy. Each one brings a fondness for who and what they have represented throughout the many Christmases shared. Children's handmade ornaments and Great-Grandma's hand-blown glass hold equal rank. I miss him putting the lights on the tree and telling me where to move one or the other. He would have liked this year's tree. That makes me smile.

For now,

Me

December

December 6, 2023

Dear Betty,

Saint Nick's soup and bread supper is over. I am glad that I decided to go through with it. It was different for sure. Doing things without my partner who always helped with some of the holiday things is rather bittersweet. While preparing the food and decorating the house I couldn't help but remember his teasing me about how I was doing things and why I was doing them. Good memories.

I have not been feeling the debilitating sadness that seemed to follow me around each and every day. Now I am feeling the other kind of sadness.

Missing his presence is the kind of feeling that creeps up on one. I am busy doing everyday chores and doing the holiday preparations when all at once I find myself missing. Missing him, missing the way things used to be, missing his help, missing his questioning just plain missing. It feels like there is a piece of me missing. Aside from the obvious, I think that there is that piece of me stuck in the grief box. Will it pop out one day and surprise me or will I suddenly realize what it was that might have been missing all along? Only time will tell, right Betty?

Happy St. Nick's Day,

Me

December 7, 2023

Dear Betty,

Last night I was sitting in the living room looking at the Christmas Tree and trying to figure out just what it was I was feeling. I landed on lonely. I was feeling lonely. Why is it so hard to admit that I am feeling lonely more times than I ever was before? Sadness, feeling lost and afraid are emotions that I felt very comfortable writing about. Lonely not so much. In order to help me find some understanding around this issue I resorted to the tool I most often use. I looked up the definition.

Loneliness is "an unpleasant response to ... " I agree with the line that says it is unpleasant. I do not feel especially isolated, however. For me, the unpleasant feeling or emotion is just unease. I feel antsy, not settled or calm.

The definition goes on to say that loneliness is associated with a lack of connection and intimacy. Now we are getting somewhere. I definitely miss the way Don and I connected. I guess it comes with a very long-term relationship. You know, Betty, the kind where partners can communicate with just a look across a crowded room or being able to finish one another's sentences. As for intimacy, it is the main source of my loneliness. It is the quick kisses when coming or going or holding hands or just being quiet in the same room together.

Loneliness is distinct from solitude. Solitude is simply the state of being apart from others; not everyone who experiences solitude feels lonely. I totally agree with this part of the definition. I enjoy my solitude. I always have. I am happy and comfortable being alone in the quiet, whether it is on a long walk or sitting on the porch or simply taking a breath and a break from whatever is around me at the time.

Have you ever felt alone or lonely in a room of people? I have and remembering this has helped me answer the question that I started with today.

When I figure out what it is that I am missing I feel less lonely. I come around to acceptance or what is currently a popular state of being "in the present moment." Missing I think is not the same as loneliness but can be the cause of loneliness.

Why do I find it hard to admit that I am lonely? Well, Betty, I think it is because old tapes play frequently in my head. 'Here we go, I should be stronger than this, I should get up and do something about this.' I can't admit that I am not perfect or completely happy all of the time.

I need to believe and accept my humanness.

I need to practice all of the lessons that I have presented to other women.

How silly of me to not know that I would have to use them someday for myself. Oh well, Betty, silly, silly me.

Soon,

Me

December 8, 2023

Dear Betty,

When did this grieving process begin? Of course, the deepest sense of grief can be pinpointed to the day he died and the time immediately following that day. Recently, however, I have been thinking about all of the things in the grief box. Now I can say that I have been in several stages of grief for some time, maybe years.

It makes sense, doesn't it? We experience loss from the moment we are born. Every stage and relationship we pass through in our lives hold change. Can we experience change without loss? I think not. As we age or you might prefer to grow, we are sad when we leave our childhood friends, we might be angry when we don't get the job we wanted or are hurt in a relationship. Along the way we probably come to some form of acceptance for our life, our age, our lot in life.

Because Don was sick for some time, I think I was and still am grieving all of the things that make up a long-term relationship. I am sad but really not regretful. I feel like we had a good, challenging, ever-changing life together. It was good.

I miss the way he could be at peace in his silence and our simple way of communicating. He had a unique personality and one that made him interesting and human. He was always loving.

So, Betty, today I grieve the past energy I had for the seasons. Christmas and another year seem a long way off even though I know it will happen in a couple of weeks with or without me. I am grateful for the memories of Christmas past and for the joy that he shared with all of us. No restrictions about what should be in or not in the grief box.

Happy Holidays,

Me

December 10, 2023

Dear Betty,

Today is a blank canvas. I am feeling rather blank. No agenda, no have to's, and no incentive to do much of anything. As I said, "blank."

Oh, I know that I will find things to do. I already finished packing the girls' Christmas bags, let the dog out, and drank my coffee while watching *Sunday Morning* on CBS. I spent too much time reviewing books on Amazon but didn't fall into the deep hole of buying any of them. I did make a list of the more interesting ones that I may read some other time. Christmas seems far away and yet it is only a couple of weeks away. I can't say that I am excited about it but neither am I wanting to deny it. Yep, blank.

I watched two Mary Higgins Clark mysteries on Amazon Prime the other day because I just didn't want to watch another formula Christmas movie. I am not dissing the Christmas movies; actually some of them have been fun to watch, even meaningful. Some of them remind me of another loss. We loved to shop for the kids together and finish the day or evening off with a quiet dinner out.

Guess I will go and do my ordinary thing for today. I am going to empty the dishwasher. Yeah me!

Be well,

Me

December 12, 2023

Dear Betty,

Where do memories come from? In the same way that I store my grief feelings in my imaginary grief box, I suppose that there is a memory box somewhere in our brains that becomes our memory file. I am not talking about the ordinary, everyday memories or the issues that we all have as we age, like remembering where we left our phones or our glasses or our car keys. I am talking about the memories that just pop into our consciousness when we take time to reflect on our lives. They pop up when we least expect them to, triggered by something someone said or something we read or while watching a holiday movie. I am sure that there are lots of scientific reasons and lots of articles that I could chase down, but I am just not inclined to do that now. I prefer just pondering this latest question and supposing my own answers.

I have noticed that my memory recall has changed. For these past months when thinking about Don the image of him has been his last days or weeks. It was of him in pain or silent and diminished, weak but doing his best and fighting each day. Recently, when I think about him, all of the time, his memory, his image, is the man who was healthy, active, and present in his own way.

I woke out of a dream this morning. In my dream, the phone rang and I answered it and it was Don. He said, "Hi honey." It was good to hear his voice.

I will put my happy feeling into my grief box and I hope that this memory will surface again and again out of the memory box in my head or maybe these kinds of memories come from our hearts. He is always on my mind.

Be happy,

Me

December 12, 2023

Dear Betty,

Wow, Betty, two letters in one day. This should be short and sweet. Well, at least short. Here I was feeling so proud of myself these last few days spouting off heady hypotheses about memory and grief. Well, again I am a fraud.

I called the insurance agent for the homeowners' insurance. He said, "Hello." I said, "I am looking for Jim." He said, "Speaking." I said, "This is Mary Bub and Don died on September sixth. I need—" and then I lost it. I really lost it, tears and sobbing. The poor guy didn't know what to say. I recovered and finished my business and he was very kind. What the hell, Betty! Grief is a mean and sneaky companion and I would like it to be gone.

Sad again,

Me

December 13, 2023

Dear Betty,

I am making French bread today. I am finally feeling like I want to do something creative again. Tess is having a party tonight and I offered to make her some bread. It feels good to get my hands in the dough. There are ideas floating around in my head that I think I may want to paint. It is a start. Maybe I will get back to enjoying being in my studio one of these days.

Yesterday was a hard day. I don't like the word acceptance. I know that I have used it in the past, encouraged others to be it, and it is something that we all bump against from time to time. Reality is the word that I am choosing to use instead. What is my reality now and how will I recognize it AND what will I do with it? So many questions and so few answers.

Each day I sit down to write to you asking myself, "What in the world can I say today?" Then when I allow myself to face the questions here, I am telling you all about what I am thinking and feeling. What a strange place to be at this time of my life. I guess I hadn't thought about it much, I must have just accepted where I was at the time. Go figure!

Funny,

Me

December 14, 2023

Dear Betty,

This morning I found myself reflecting on my letter to you yesterday. I am sure you have noticed I often fight against the things that I don't want to deal with. Maybe I don't want to face whatever reality is staring me in the face.

What does avoidance have to do with my stubborn need to ignore the word or behavior of acceptance? Here is where I am right in the middle of the question. Of course, I have accepted the fact that Don is gone. He is no longer physically present. For some time, I thought that he would come walking back into the house from the garden or that he would have an opinion about my cooking from the living room. He is gone. I will, I am sure, continue to hear his voice offering his advice about many things.

What is it I don't want to accept? What am I avoiding? Admitting that his quiet spirit and his old and wise soul are gone, this is the problem. But are they? I think not. No, I will not accept that the essence of him is completely out of my life. I do still hear his voice and remember his way of being. I hope that I never lose these things. Good, bad, happy, sad, this was our life and I am ever grateful that he chose to share his with me. I choose to avoid total acceptance of his absence. Rather, I choose to hold to what was most meaningful, authentic, and true for us.

One of the meanings of acceptance is "to welcome" or "welcoming." What I welcome are the memories that I hold dear and listening to the family share their memories as well. I especially like the humorous ones.

Till then,

Me

December 17, 2023

Dear Betty,

Accomplished my first-ever funeral as the officiant. It went well but it was both emotionally and physically draining. It took yesterday to process and recover.

Now I want to ponder the differences between happiness and being content. I also need to figure out why I am feeling so crappy today. I really enjoy gifting people, not just during the holidays but whenever. What I am cranky about today is that someone calls and asks for the gift that I make and that they want. I suppose that I should be glad that they like my homemade gifts, maybe even appreciate the fact that they asked. It just made me cranky. Maybe I am too settled in my grieving process and too selfish to be disturbed by something that I don't want to do. Not feeling a really giving spirit.

Guess I have to add crappy and generous to the grief box. I need to get rid of one and practice the other.

Next time,

Me

December 19, 2023

Dear Betty,

Confessions are hard. I am confessing that I didn't write to you yesterday and I have no good reason for not doing so. The grief box offered me a good helping of self-doubt. I thought about what I wrote, declaring that I was going to ponder the differences between happiness and being content. This brought me around to wondering if anything that I have shared with you has any relevance at all. Maybe I am just playing with words. As you know I have done word play most of my adult life.

There are so many books and articles about happiness. So many experts tell us that we should be happy, that when grieving we should know that there will be happiness again. Then there are the authors who, out of their vast experience of maybe 25 years, "think they can teach us" how to be happy, gain happiness, get happy, etc …

Just what has the 20th century taught us about being happy? Maybe the folks who lived through the Great Depression didn't have much, but it seems to me that they had a deeper sense of happiness. My family had little but they had much in that they shared what they did have. They laughed and played and taught their children how to be good people.

I am waiting for the day when I will say, "That made me happy." I don't know what that thing will be that will cause my soul to respond, but I am trying to stay open to the possibility. So, what was I thinking about being content? Is it just another way of saying I am experiencing some amount of acceptance? No, that doesn't cut it for me. Content, comfortable in my waiting. There might be a definition that I can live with for a while. Most of my days are spent feeling at peace with the sadness and the missing. Perhaps this is as content as I can be until by some overwhelming grace, I am happy again.

Sadly yours,

Me

December 20, 2023

Dear Betty,

My lunch date was canceled today. This is both disappointing and a relief. Of course, I miss seeing my friend and talking to her in person, but we did have a great morning of coffee and robes. Now I don't have to hurry to get everything ready for our Kindred's gathering tomorrow.

I am tired today. No good reason that I can think of. It makes me wonder if my feeling of contentment is waning. Is this a harbinger of yet another level of sadness? I am probably reading too much into it and letting fear push me into the depths of the grief box. Maybe I am just tired because of all of the things that have happened in the past several weeks and I am just now feeling the effects. That is where I am settling my mind today.

Missing, Betty. Just what is missing? Obviously, it is the absence of someone or something but still, what does it feel like? How does one act when the missing stalks your being just waiting for an opening to bring you to tears?

I think that allowing the missing can lead to an understanding of what my life might look like now and in the future. It is not denying the feeling. Could it be one step to coming to acceptance? Or the kind of contentment that says, this is your reality but I can do this and still be settled and quiet in myself? More than one way to feel content, do you think?

Caring,

Me

December 26, 2023

Dear Betty,

Can it really be? I cannot believe that it has been six days since I wrote to you. Losing days must be another sign of what happens in this ongoing saga named grief. But still, six days? Recalling just what consumed those days seems difficult. I know that I went shopping half-heartedly with Christy one day. Laura spent a couple of days here baking Christmas cookies. We did watch several Christmas movies so I guess that accounts for some of the time. Time is too fleeting to forget. It is not something that I want to lose.

Today I am pondering the last two days of Christmas. Christmas Eve day was a day for the grief box to celebrate. It provided so many emotions—emotions that caught me by surprise and emotions that made me even more leery of recounting memories. I felt alone and vulnerable.

Why is it that I react to someone being nice to me? The phrase, "How are you doing?" can set me off in a minute. Then I feel embarrassed but Betty, when the follow-up remark is, "It's OK to be vulnerable with us" something in me fights back. It's not like I chose to have tears flowing down my checks every other minute.

So here is my dilemma, one of my life goals is to be authentic. Well, then, it follows that I should be willing to let my vulnerability show. It is after all what I am feeling at the moment.

I have come to wonder if it is all about expectations. The expectations that I have for myself and the expectations that others might have of me. At my age, I am told that I am the elder, the wise one, the matriarch. Is stuffing my feelings or showing my embarrassment being a good example? At this point, I tend to want to say, who cares anyway?

Betty, I must admit that I did not do a good job of preparing myself for the family gathering. Probably because I didn't write to you for six days and get my head on straight. Maybe I was afraid of memories of Christmas past. Who knows, I sure don't.

Another observance. It seems to me that my grandsons are more empathetic to me than the girls. I received lovely hugs from the boys. Not big showy hugs but the kind that just say, love you and I am here too. I don't want to say that the girls are not caring, I am more inclined to think that they are not sure about how to handle their own feelings.

Another Christmas has passed now and I am adding expectations to the grief box.

I am pretty sure that I have already fussed about vulnerability so will just continue to be present to it when needs be.

Hope to do better,

Me

December 27, 2023

Dear Betty,

Embarrassed. After my missive of yesterday I began to wonder just what it is that makes me veer away from showing my vulnerability. I have come to the conclusion, at least for now, that I don't want to feel embarrassed. Of course, this means that I am admitting my need to be "together, on top of things, in control." What is it I would be embarrassed about? Perhaps my inability to control my emotions. To let others see me as needy.

So, Betty, it all comes back to expectations. Has all of the work I have done on self-awareness through all of these years been for naught? No, I know that buried deep down inside me it is all still there. It has been displaced by this nagging grief. It has taken over all of my senses. I feel senseless.

Have to run, more later,

Me

December 28, 2023

Dear Betty,

Plans for today have been canceled. Probably just as well as I didn't sleep well last night and I feel perfectly happy to have a quiet day at home. It is cold and cloudy but it was snowing early this morning. It was snow globe snow and it made me smile.

Now it is just slushy and wet. Maybe this is how I feel today. Washed out, tear-stained without a smile. Boy, doesn't that sound like poor me? Still, I am struggling to be honest and present to the moment/day. Might be a good day for a nap.

I am still thinking about being vulnerable and embarrassed. Do you think it might be akin to feeling like I have wounded my pride if I expose feelings? Pride: "self-esteem, dignity, self-respect, ego, self-image, pride in one's abilities, faith in oneself." This is quite a list. I have worked hard to achieve these qualities so I can see that I don't want to let them go. OK here I am again thinking that if I thought that I had lost any of them I would be embarrassed. On the other hand, I know full well that letting ego get in the way can prevent me from being the person I want to be. How does one have a healthy ego in the midst of the grieving process? Should this even be a question?

Perhaps if I have faith in myself, a little bit of ego or a healthy one might just allow me to take another step toward my goal of being authentic. Betty, I think that I have just gone around the block and come out back in the place of enjoying a small moment of awareness. I think I would be wise to stop here for today.

Last word—grief is a tough task master/mistress.

Be well,

Me

December 29, 2023

Dear Betty,

Last night I was thinking about the feelings that I have encountered in the course of this journey. More of them than I would have considered before grief took center stage.

An image that came to mind was a merry-go-round. All of the horses and carriages going round and round, up and down. It seems like that is exactly what I feel like. Sometimes I feel up, telling myself that it is a good day and I am making progress towards "what is coming next." Then my pony goes down and around and I am back, not to the very beginning, but not yet at the end of the ride.

I am trying to get in touch with what I am feeling today. First of all, it is really gloomy outside my window. Foggy, too. I could cheat and say "Yep, that is what I am feeling." Honestly, though, I think that what I am really feeling is dull. I feel like I have lost my shine. Nothing glittery about me today. No sense of excitement about the upcoming New Year's Eve Party or the new year in general. No shine at all.

Maybe it is OK to just ride my pretty little pony round and round for a while.

I think that I will know when it is time to get off the merry-go-round and continue on my journey.

Who knows?

Always,

Me

December 30, 2023

Dear Betty,

While trying to identify my feelings or just what it is that I am feeling, a new phrase came to mind. I am feeling blue. 'What does that mean?' I said to myself.

What I discovered are some facts that really do not help me articulate my condition but were interesting nonetheless. Its origin is either found in the 1300s or the 17th century. It is just another way of saying that one is sad or melancholy. The definition that held the most meaning for me was from the 1300s that said to be blue or feeling blue is the result of lack of oxygen.

Early on in the grief process I did feel at times like I couldn't breathe. Not literally, of course, because of course I was breathing, but I was feeling a deeper sense of not being able to catch my breath. I felt like I lacked oxygen. I couldn't think or reason. Everything felt surreal. Now I feel like I can't breathe emotionally. Feelings take my breath away and still I try to remember to acknowledge the pain of sadness and breathe.

Today, I am breathing, there is oxygen fueling my brain, and my mood is not as blue as the night sky. I am feeling blue (sad) but the shade of blue is lightening at times. I even find myself saying, "I am in the mood for ..."

We'll see what tomorrow brings. Oh my, that almost sounds like the beginning of hope.

Gratefully,

Me

December 31, 2023

Dear Betty,

This last week has been difficult. I am sure you realize that from my letters. I have been wrestling with my decision to go to the New Year's Eve party or not.

The thought of going out on a cold snowy dark winter night just doesn't seem like what I want to do. But truthfully, it is not the weather that wants to keep me home—it is the opening of the grief box and accepting its message. What message might you ask? Here goes—the message is, "It is OK to stay home. It is OK to not want to be around a large group of people, some of whom I don't even know."

As I have been told many times lately, it is alright to choose what is right for you, you are grieving. As though I don't know that! I will prepare the food that I promised but I will stay home tonight.

Some new ideas also fell out of the g box. I heard an interview on TV this morning. The upshot of it was someone saying that he had stuffed, ignored, and just not dealt with his grief for most of his life. There are certainly days that I want to stuff my grief and some other things, too. Usually, though, I come back to my natural instincts of dealing with my emotional self. Finally, he said that he was going to work on his buried grief.

This gave me pause to think about my own grief in a new way. What if I try to nurture my grief rather than just keep trying to name it every day? What might it mean to nurture my grief? What does it mean to nurture? I like the idea of attending to it or to bring it up like a child at the very least, paying attention to it. I want to explore what mature grief might look like. I think that I will try to nurture my grief. Pay attention to it and hopefully come to some understanding of what growing to mature grief might be.

Happy New Year, Betty,

Me

JANUARY

January 1, 2024

Dear Betty,

After just telling you in yesterday's letter that maybe I don't have to name my feelings each day I came across this quote from the American Behavioral Clinics. *"Emotionally mature people observe their thoughts and feelings in order to effectively manage, communicate, and cope with difficult emotions. Emotional maturity is more than being able to maintain your composure. It's also: understanding what you're feeling. being able to show emotions in a healthy way."*

Maybe I could use this definition as a map to mature grief. Is observing my thoughts and feelings different from naming them? I would sure like to be able to manage, communicate, and cope with them. I am beginning to think that mature grief is coming to some kind of understanding about what I am feeling and then managing my emotions in a healthy way. Maybe managing mature grief is not so much about maintaining my composure but learning what to do with what lessons I might glean along the way.

This reflection brings me back to the idea of nurturing my grief. While thinking about it last night in the quiet, I started to play with the idea that if I am to nurture it, to attend to it, or to bring it up and care for it I would have to know at what stage of development it might be. I don't want to get entangled in the overused five stages of grief, but, rather, look at grief more developmentally. I have concluded that I have experienced two of three stages as I define them.

The first is Chaos, the time immediately after the loss. Nothing seems reasonable, thoughts get jumbled, memory is foggy at best, there are too many emotions to deal with all at once.

The second is Impulsive. In this stage, where by the way is where I think I am now, I feel like my emotions are acting impulsively, surfacing at any time and most times not even making me feel that I can define why. They are spontaneous and uninhibited. Ah, Betty, I bet you want to know what the third stage might be. Me too. I am hoping that it will be quiet, assured Awareness.

So today I am regretfully naming my feelings as sad, a little depressed, and missing which I have decided is different from lonely. I am not feeling alone or lonely but I am missing Don's presence and his love.

Best to you in 2024,

Me

January 2, 2024

Dear Betty,

Today I am coming to the conclusion that I have been nurturing my grief all along. I have been attending to it and hopefully doing things that will find me in mature grief. Forcing myself to be aware of what the grief box is offering me each day and trying my best to articulate its meaning to myself has been my way of nurturing.

My ordinary thing today was rather fulfilling. I went to the post office and mailed a gift box off to my dear friend who I send a little Christmas present to each year. Then I had lunch with my daughter and enjoyed some really good conversation. She is a kind and caring woman and I love spending time with her.

So, Betty, what am I feeling today? A bit tired and glad that the holidays are over. I am looking forward to moving into the new year with purpose and direction. At least, that is my hope.

Till then,

Me

January 3, 2024

Dear Betty,

This morning I woke up with the word resignation on my mind. It means, along with other things, a sad feeling of accepting something because you cannot really change it. Upon reflection, I realize that I am not resigned to my grief. I do believe it will change and that if I continue accepting my process it will. I am, however, determined. I am doing my best to be decisive and resolute when it comes to accepting whatever comes out of the grief box.

One of the most difficult things that I hope to be determined about is accepting the truth that time will have her way with me. I strive to learn that there can be peace in silence and that when the time is right, my determination to stay in my process will be fruitful. I am grateful for the time I had with Don while waiting, waiting for an appointment, waiting for results, waiting for the doctor, just waiting. I wouldn't have thought that his patience with the waiting would serve me well now.

It is really cold and dark today, Betty. Winter is upon us.

Be warm,

Me

January 4, 2024

Dear Betty,

Back to ordinary things. I went to East Troy today and had a haircut. Funny how a simple thing like getting my haircut makes me feel fresh and happy. The sun was out this morning and it too made me happy. Plans that I had for the rest of the day were canceled and now I find myself at loose ends. Back to the silence.

Do you think that I can manage two ordinary things today? I do. I think I will do some laundry and just maybe I will go to the studio for a bit.

I feel the salty wetness waiting just behind my eyes, but so far they are not forming drops and wetting my cheeks. I take this to be a good day.

York is patiently waiting for me to take him outside for his morning "catch the frisbee" time. Another ordinary thing. I guess that is the order of the day. Just staying with the ordinary somehow feels right and good.

Bye Betty,

Me

January 6, 2024

Dear Betty,

I woke up this morning after a restless night with a lot of "shoulds" in my mind. I went out yesterday to visit a friend and when I came home, I started to take down the holiday decorations. In the midst of this busyness, I forgot about all of the other things that I was going to do. Not sure that I will tackle any of them today either.

It felt good to visit with my friend. As I was driving home, I wondered if it is possible to be sad and happy at the same time. I think I have asked this question before but here it is again. I am not even sure that happy is the right word; maybe calm or content would be better.

Another thought for today—there are so many more things in the grief box than I would have imagined.

Like what, you might ask? Like appreciation. I am so appreciative of the time I had to love and be loved. I am so appreciative for all of those people who comforted and supported me these past years and who continue to grace me still today. So, I am adding appreciation to the g box.

It is cold and snowy today and I am going to stay in, eat comfort food, and spend some time in my cozy chair. Maybe a good movie is warranted.

Gratefully,

Me

January 7, 2024

Dear Betty,

So here is my metaphor for today. It is cloudy today but the sun is trying its best to show his face and lighten up the day. I am feeling restless today. I did some writing and I did the ordinary morning things. The clouds that surround my emotions are beginning to lighten because the sun is in there somewhere. What is interesting about this is that I am not crabby waiting for it to shine, but rather, I am watching for it hopefully.

Not much else to say today. Doing my best to find peace in my silence.

Almost shining,

Me

January 8, 2024

Dear Betty,

They say that all of the firsts are bad. I am not so sure about this because it seems like I am still in the throes of living an ongoing surreal reality. Tomorrow we are forecasted to have a major snowstorm. It will be the first of this winter. There are so many memories connected to winter snowstorms. Listening to the weather forecasts for days ahead of the storm, waiting for it to begin, and then watching it come down. Somehow it is Mother Nature's way of asserting herself.

It seems my mood has changed from feeling restless yesterday to feeling resigned today. To be fair, though, it does seem like these mood swings and days of feeling lost are not so much like building blocks piling one on top of the other, but more like waves of recognition begging me to challenge myself to name them when I just want to sit and wait for the storm that may bring with it a new landscape.

I just realized, Betty, that I have created a metaphor for exactly how I have been feeling now; another way to describe the journey I have been living. We listened to so many doctors and nurses give us the forecast for the future. Then we waited and tried our best to do our best together. Then the storm came, and for a while, there were quiet and calm moments. As much as I regret saying it, there was some beauty in living through the storm. Like the fresh fallen snow, it was clean and soft because we weathered it together in our way.

Deep in this second stage of grief, I find myself able to see between the tears the goodness of it. What I would have missed had I not been his partner on his journey, on our journey, together. Betty, I miss him so!

Be you and be well,

Me

January 10, 2024

Dear Betty,

Some time ago I confessed to feeling lost. Today I am once again focusing on the word lost as it is the one I picked blindly out of the grief box. I am not thinking or perhaps feeling about it as lost and lonely but rather in reference to the things that I feel that I have lost.

Yes, I have lost my husband, my partner, at times my mentor, and always my friend. Yet, recently I, while trying to come to grips with whatever I am feeling on any given day, have come around to asking myself, 'What part of me have I lost?'

Some of my identifiers have remained: mother, grandmother, great-grandmother, and friend. I feel as though I have lost an amount of self-esteem. Where is my motivation? I am not feeling terribly creative, either.

I am passionate or maybe even getting too passion-ate about our cultural view of aging. One of the biggies is my sense of self-image. This makes me reject doing some of the things that I might have thought of doing or that I have done in the past. How will others view me? I am clearly old. I have the body of an older person but my mind doesn't seem to go there.

Part of my identity for many, many years was as a wife, and as Don would say often, "Just talk to her, she is my secretary." I didn't mind this. I knew he appreciated my helping with his appointments. I am not sure, however, that I have settled into the "widow" role. I also find myself realizing that I am an orphan. Just more reminders that life is a journey and no matter how much we deny it, truth in this matter wins out.

Till then,

Me

January 11, 2024

Dear Betty,

Trees glistening outside of my window make me wonder if I am starting to get my shine back. Some days I feel pretty shiny, others not so much. While I am thinking about what I have lost, perhaps I should also try to identify what I have gained. Where is my new shine? Do I have more under-standing, am I gaining wisdom, do I see things with more clarity now? Maybe what I have lost is some of the clatter then, as the "Desiderata" says, "noise and haste."

Inconsequential is a word that I have been pon-dering. Maybe some of the things that I think I have lost were after all inconsequential. I may have needed them, even worked hard at gaining them, teaching other women all about the selves. Self-care, self-nourishing, self-awareness, self-es-teem and all of the others. I am definitely still work-ing hard on self-awareness and I am doing my best to take care of myself. But the constant effort for many other selves seems inconsequential. In the song *Amazing Grace*, we all sing, "I was lost but now I am found, was blind but now I see." Betty, I agree!

At times lately I feel inconsequential. What of me matters? Some of who I was and what I did seems far away and long ago. So now I am back to fo-cusing on the roles I have played over the last few years. Both here at home with my partner and in the world of community. If I can find the relevant pieces of me now during this part of my life's journey then I will know that my life, my self, is not inconsequential. And neither is yours, Betty!

Full of grace,

Me

January 13, 2024

Dear Betty,

We had a snowstorm, well really it was a blizzard, yesterday. We haven't had one of those in several years. I didn't write yesterday because truthfully, I didn't want to name my feelings and I didn't want to think. Today I am ready to fess up to a barrage of feelings. In some ways the snowstorm was exciting. Watching the power of Mother Nature in winter mode made me small in the power and scope of all that was happening. I was also in awe of the beauty of this thing that was both throwing our quiet countryside into chaos and turning it at the same time into a picture postcard.

The grief box delivered feelings of melancholy, another day of missing. I could hear Don's voice commenting on the storm. I could hear him telling me not to worry. That we were safe and that we would weather the storm. Aren't those interesting words? They brought tears to my eyes because I was feeling blue and wondered if, in fact, I would weather this grief-filled emotional storm.

What got me out of my funk? Or should I say what moved me to some understanding and to a more comfortable feeling place? I let myself go to the place of remembering all of the storms that we have weathered. Ultimately, my word for today is gratitude. Smiles were even apparent on my face last night as I thought about all of the times we shoveled snow together and celebrated with a good cup of hot cocoa. I can smile now, as well, knowing that even through the stormy times we managed together. The sun came out today.

Shining,

Me

January 14, 2024

Dear Betty,

It is cold and frigid. The sun did come out today though and somehow that makes it a little better. These past few days have found me with my sad exposed. There are so many memories bouncing around my head. Snowstorms were both difficult times and fun times for our family. Another fickle memory. I didn't sleep well last night, too many worries and listening to the not-so-friendly wind whistling around the house.

The grief box likes to pop open when I am tired and don't want to face the emotions floating just under the surface. I find it frustrating that during these times when all I want is to rest and to have a quiet mind I am back into the months and the last year. Once again asking the questions that I already know the answers to and having to work hard at remembering the time before.

Today will be a day for finding distractions and hoping for a good night's sleep.

Stay warm,

Me

January 17, 2024

Dear Betty,

Tomorrow is my birthday. I wonder if I will feel any different about my age than I do now. I have been very aware lately of how much I need to get out, socialize, and listen to someone else's voice besides mine. But just because I know this about myself now, I am still not motivated to do anything about it. Oh, I know, Betty, there are plenty of things that I could do. After all, I have years of learning and experiences to share. I could do something helpful, like volunteering at the food pantry. What stops me? My major excuse is, I am not in a good place and not ready to share my thoughts and feelings. I am old and who would want to take me seriously anyway?

There are mountains of snow all around the house. I feel like I am stuck in the middle of one of them. The world around me is lovely, glistening in the sun. I am trying not to struggle to get out, but rather trying to stay in the process. It is uncomfortable and I wake most mornings wondering if today is the day that I will not feel this veil of yesterday surrounding me.

We never did much to celebrate our birthdays. We did celebrate our children's birthdays, though. One thing I will miss tomorrow is Don singing "Happy Birthday" to me several times during the day. It

was his one special thing to do for everyone in the
family.

Another month, another day, another year.

Make a snowman,

Me

January 18, 2024

Dear Betty,

I made it. My 80th birthday and the sun is shining. I have the Kindreds meeting here today and looking forward to celebrating with them. There are three of us celebrating birthdays today.

Feeling pleased today because I am prepared for the conversation and I really enjoy this small group of women. I want to tell you that I am happy. Happy seems like too big of a word. Maybe content or calm would be better. Excited is definitely not how I feel today.

What will this year bring? When I got up today my first thought was, "What will this year bring?" Really, Betty, I am hoping that before we get too far into 2024, I will find out what the third stage will be and how it will feel.

Trying to celebrate today,

Me

January 19, 2024

Dear Betty,

Made it through to the other side of the birthday celebration. Enjoying the quiet today and feeling very grateful for all of the good wishes of yesterday. One of my big surprises was the delivery of a beautiful basket of spring flowers from my favorite flower shop. They were from my friend Lis and totally unexpected. Then this morning I opened the front door to check out how much snow we got overnight and there was a box waiting for me. It was from Dre. Inside there were two homespun angels. One taller and one considerably smaller. They reminded me of the two of us as Dre is much taller than I am. Both of these gifts were so unexpected, made me smile, and made my heart happy.

Glad,

Me

January 20, 2024

Dear Betty,

Today I added expectations to the grief box. I realize now that expectations are just a part of who I am. Aren't they part of everyone? Maybe this is one way to decide if we are optimists or pessimists. Having expectations can also bar the door to living in the present moment. As I travel my own personal grief road, I think that I am quietly and secretly expecting that my life will feel better. I expect that I will do things and be things just like I always have done and been.

Of course, I know that my life is everchanging. I know that my age alone creates a different kind of expectation. How I approach my role as mother, grandmother and even great-grandmother has changed more quickly than I would want it to.

Yesterday I celebrated my birthday without much thought to what my expectations might be for the coming year. I pushed any feelings of grieving my aging self aside and strolled through the day distracting myself with a mediocre TV movie. I wonder when I gave up having expectations of what we would do together. I don't think that our end-of-life plans could be named expectations. They were, gratefully, a thoughtful and good thing that we did together.

Betty, for the first time in so many years I do not feel in control or that I have any sense of direction or understanding about what might lie ahead. I do expect that I will get back some of my old self and that I will learn to acquaint myself with the new me that I grow into.

With Expectations,

Me

January 21, 2024

Dear Betty,

Didn't sleep very well last night and woke early this morning. The house seems especially quiet this morning. I am feeling the lonely side of sad. This often happens when I am tired. I spent a nice day with my daughter yesterday. At times after a full day like that I do feel some amount of letdown. Maybe it is the part of me that wants to hold on to the full moments. I wish I could bank them for times that are not so full and I struggle to be present.

Tomorrow,

Me

January 22, 2024

Dear Betty,

Adrift, floating around untethered with no land in sight. Empty, nothing inside to pour out. Wandering, searching for the right path, to take me where? Not without hope, just without direction or encouragement. Lost and alone here in the last chapters of my life.

The light will shine tomorrow, the fog will lift, and I will see the land. It may be off in the distance, but I will be able to see it. There will be road signs or maybe a fellow traveler to point the way to the path to somewhere.

I am not lost or alone, just waiting.

Alright,

Me

January 23, 2024

Dear Betty,

"A Wish for the Week Ahead" was the title of one of those feel-good posts on Facebook. I read it thinking that I could use a good wish. The first line read, "May you look for the good in an increasingly complicated reality." No doubt about that, I thought. It went on to remind the reader that they have goodness inside just waiting to be shared with a world that desperately needs it. Well, maybe there is still goodness inside of me but it may be overwhelmed by all of the other feelings rambling around in there. Does the world need my goodness or do I have to find it first?

"Keep taking steps toward your goals," it said. "What goals?!" I shouted at the screen. I hardly know what I might be doing on any given day, even finding one ordinary thing can sometimes be daunting. "Forgive yourself when you falter as you inevitably will." Thanks a lot, I thought. Nothing like laying a guilt trip on an already vulnerable poor little me. "Face your challenges with courage and kindness." This reminded me of the calls or cards that I have received that encourage me to remember that I am resilient, that I can do this, that I will come out on the other side. What side is that? I wonder.

About resilience. I have always thought of myself that way but now I wonder if I am truly resilient or am I just stubborn. Am I just too determined to get it "right?" Do I have to prove to myself and others that I am not going to be one of "those" weeping willows? Betty, my friend, all of this reflection has brought me back to, yes, one of my long-time goals. I do want to be authentic in myself and in what I do. It is just so damn hard to let down the armor, the persona, that I have carried for all of these years. My sweet prince knew me, saw through the armor, and gently helped me to be. I miss him.

Quite a ramble today, Betty. I do think that some of these invitations to self-care that appear on Facebook are helpful. In the end, it was helpful to me today.

With caring,

Me

January 24, 2024

Dear Betty,

It is a dreary, foggy day and a good metaphor for how I am feeling. Recently, at our monthly gathering, we were talking about the difference between loneliness and being alone. Most of us said that we enjoyed being alone at times. Now that might be a clue. At times.

One of the women asked me, if I was lonely would I reach out to someone? I quickly replied, "No, I don't think that I am lonely, I try to think about what I am missing." Well, that was a week ago and I have been thinking about how I responded to her question. I have come to the conclusion that if I am missing someone or something that I am lonely. Why? Because it or them is missing, not there, not here. It is a different kind of lonely. It is a heartache and not one that can be helped by reaching out to anyone.

Yes, generally if we are lonely and we reach out to a friend or family member and ask them to have lunch or if we join a club or group of some kind, we may not feel as lonely. But Betty, the kind of lonely that comes out of the grief box is its own kind of pain, sadness, and wish-you-were-here kind.

So, I am lonely sometimes. I am missing all of the things that had become familiar to our relationship, the way we were together, the growing together, the angst we caused one another, the laughter and the tears. I am missing his love.

Brighter skies tomorrow,

Me

January 25, 2024

Dear Betty,

Skies are not brighter today but my mood is. It is Don's birthday today. I thought that I would be especially sad today but I am only usually sad. We celebrated many birthdays together. Some of them memorable and some of them just another ordinary day. Happy Birthday, Don.

I was listening to a program this morning and the word "content" came up. Oh boy, I thought, another word for the grief box. What does it mean for me? When was the last time I felt content? I feel like I have been pretty content with my life. In many of the stages of our lives together, I have felt satisfied. Is satisfied the same as content? Maybe I think that contentment is a deeper sense of being satisfied. Maybe there are no strings attached to contentment. Just a peaceful, quiet, OK way of being. Somehow, satisfied comes to me as maybe putting up with, or not willing to take the next step to contentment.

I must say, Betty, I have had moments of feeling content. For me they were peaceful moments that may or may not have had some reaching back to moments or times of deep knowing that all was well.

Can one feel contentment and worry or regret at the same time? Grabbing at moments of feeling content encourages me to let go of worry, especially the unfounded kind, and to let go of regret for what is certainly now in the rearview mirror.

Can reaching out for contentment be a goal? Or perhaps it is a wish or a longing that in time will replace some of the unease that comes with the grief box.

Be content today, Betty,

Me

January 27, 2024

Dear Betty,

I saw the sun for, oh, I don't know, maybe a minute or two. It made my heart happy and I thought, today the sun was a gift. Although there are so many gloomy and foggy days this winter and in this winter of my heart, just having these precious moments reminds me that the sun will shine again. I will shine again.

I have been trying to listen to the words of authors and spiritual leaders that I have had respect for in the past. I still respect them but somehow I want new words. I need new words. Writing to you, Betty, has helped me to think of my authentic words. The words and experiences like seeing the sun this morning are the things that give me hope these days.

Today we are having the family January birthday party. I have been making bread for the past two days. The words I have heard are Don asking me "What are you doing? What are you making?" When seeing the finished product, he would have said, "That looks good."

Funny thing, Betty, I went up to the studio yesterday and did a painting of the ocean from our visit to Gold Beach. I heard his voice saying the exact same things he said about the bread repeated about the painting. I hope that I never forget these moments or the sound of his voice.

The word that I am not sure I think about or hear is still "unpredictable." I breezed through last Thursday, Don's birthday. I was pleased with myself and I wondered if I had taken another step to step three, whatever that may be. Well, I am sure that you would say, beware—you are not there yet. Sure enough, the very next day every little thing brought the old grief box off of the shelf and I was almost beside myself with sadness.

Today the sun blessed me,

Me

January 28, 2024

Dear Betty,

All around me life just keeps on keeping on. The birthdays keep coming, the date on the calendar changes, weekends turn into weeks, and I am the only one who can decide who I want to be and what I want to do. I haven't a clue.

I have spent a good share of my life trying to answer these questions. Now it seems that they are not as important as I thought them to be. In an old episode of *Mash,* an old TV series, they asked a man, "Who are you?" He pointed to himself and said, "I am me." I think that I will respond to my own question in the same way. After all, I am me. All that I am, all that I have been, and even as the years roll by, I will still be me.

Sure, feelings change, there are physical changes, relationships change, and I have a new title to add to mother, grandmother, great-grandmother. I am a widow, and I am me.

Now I have feelings that I have not had in the same way before. Everything, all of my emotional well-being, seems deeper, closer to the surface.

What do I want to do? Be aware and authentic in myself and with all I may encounter in this stage of my life and while on this journey and beyond.

You know Betty, being me, is doing something.

Be you,

Me

January 31, 2024

Dear Betty,

Today I am feeling weary and without much incentive to do anything except ponder the day. I bet that you are tired of me saying that I am sad. I have tried to think of other words, words that I have shared with you in the past. Still, even though I know that I might fit into one of the categories of one of those words, the one that seems to sit solidly in me is sad.

It reminds me of one of the middle-of-the-night chats that we had. We sat there together on the side of the bed. I was holding his hand, neither of us was saying much, just sitting there in the softly lit room waiting. Then, he looked at me and asked, "How are you?" "Sad," I said. Still holding my hand, he said, "Me too."

I may never be able to fully understand exactly what that feeling was other than to say it was a shared moment of feeling something together. There were no other words, just voiceless knowing that we were sharing something that we had not shared before. This moment, this sadness was calm, quiet, and intimate. Just between the two of us.

So, if you ask me today, "How are you?" I will respond, "Sad, alone, and longing for a moment that I can only hold in my heart and my memory."

Be happy Betty,

Me

FEBRUARY

February 1, 2024

Dear Betty,

Back to ordinary. Today I will go to the bank and the mailbox. Then I will be sure to go to the studio and try to paint. Once again, I am finding it hard to get up some incentive to be creative.

I was thinking about my missive to you yesterday. I realize that I have probably told you more than once about my middle-of-the-night talk with Don. This led me to questioning myself about why I continue to come back to that memory. Here is what I decided was the answer. In that moment, in the dark quiet of the night, we were together. There didn't need to be any more words or explanations about why we were both feeling sad. There was just a deep sense that we understood and it didn't need any more than that.

Once again, our hearts were joined in a silent moment that has created a memory that rests deeply in my soul.

Another month, another day, another year. And so, it goes.

Be you,

Me

February 2, 2024

Dear Betty,

Recently I find myself censoring what I say and to whom I say it. Here is what happened. I was trying to work out the meaning of a word and how it affected my life, my conversations. As I shared the word, the person with whom I was sharing it, instead of listening to the words under the words proceeded to tell me how to fix a problem that I didn't think existed.

It wasn't that I wanted her to tell me how to feel or think about this word or the situation that I had shared. I just wanted some listening. Not even understanding. Just listening and letting me come to my own conclusions.

Since this has happened to me more than once lately, I have decided that because I am walking in a grief process, others think that I need help with issues that they think I could have dealt with before grief.

What do you think, Betty? I think that we have not been taught to accept death and grief as a culture. We don't know what to say or how to help if we want to and so we stop a conversation by side-stepping it or de-railing it.

Here I will stop using the collective we and say I at times don't know how to be with another person or family in grief. Hopefully I am learning some valuable lessons while proceeding down the path of this uncomfortable grief journey.

Walk with me,

Me

February 3, 2024

Dear Betty,

Appreciation. Today I am adding the word appreciate to the grief box. Last night when I was feeling pretty blue but not blue enough to reach out to anyone, I had a realization. I realized that whenever I get caught in the memories that make me tear up, I could reach into the memory bank and focus on the times and the people who I appreciate or have appreciated.

Here is what I learned about the definition of appreciate: "to grasp the worth or significance of something." Maybe I could spend some time identifying which memories I find worthy of my reflection. What is the significance of the memories that keep coming back time and time again? The next offering in the definition helps with the answer. It asks one to "value or to admire something highly." I value my friendships and there are women in my life that I admire highly. These are memories I want to tuck away safely. I want to return to them often.

"To judge with heightened perception or understanding; to be fully aware of something or someone. As I remember the times that I appreciated Don for who he was, the whole of him, I can say that my perception of how important those moments were have made me aware of how much I value and, yes Betty, miss our life together. Why, I ask myself, is this perception heightened? Perhaps it is because we think and feel differently about something or someone who is never to be with us again. I am grateful that my perception is more open and honest, and that it helps me understand and become aware of him and of who I am becoming.

Appreciate. A word that has become part of pop culture. How many times do we hear someone say, "I appreciate you"? I hear it mostly on TV talk shows. I have used it myself a few times. Is it because I sometimes like to jump into pop culture and play with new words or phrases? Of course, they are not new words but they get revived and suddenly they become a "thing." I find that to say, "I appreciate you" very useful when I want someone to know that I, for lack of a better word, do appreciate them, am grateful for them, and recognize who they are or what they have done.

I find so many times during this grief journey that words fail me. There are times when I receive a condolence from another person who I might not be close to or who is an acquaintance of another family member. They offer kind words but sometimes they offer cliches. I find it helpful to either just respond with a polite thank you or maybe even "I appreciate you." Do I appreciate them? I don't know—but I do appreciate them for taking the time to reach out to me and offer consolation.

"To recognize with gratitude." The last of the definitions is a good place for me to end this missive, Betty. It challenges me to recognize, to be aware of, the meaning of appreciate, and for that I am grateful. I hope that I will recognize with gratitude those memories that I appreciate in a whole new way.

Gratefully,

Me

February 4, 2024

Dear Betty,

I would like to be able to tell you that yesterday was a really good day. It was not! I didn't sleep well and so I am feeling frustrated with being tired. I did have the dog out for a short while in the sunshine and that lightens my mood.

The grief box feels really heavy today and I just want to ignore it, give up, pretend that all is well. It isn't and I won't.

Trying,

Me

February 6, 2024

Dear Betty,

I was brave today. I went to the funeral home and made all of the arrangements for my own funeral. It feels good to have it taken care of so that my children don't have to worry about it or be surprised when I leave them to take care of my final needs. I was surprised at how comfortable I was with the whole process. Of course, it was a great help that Dan is a friend. He was so helpful when we celebrated Don and Geri. His own father is dying and still he was compassionate and professional all at the same time.

In the course of our conversation, I mentioned that I would be willing to help with memorial services for those who do not have an officiant. He was happy for the offer and asked if I would be willing to offer the service if it was not pro bono. I surprised myself for the second time today and answered yes without a second thought. Maybe this is the door that I have been waiting to open. Or not. But still, I am grateful for this little while of feeling both brave and surprised.

Another thought, Betty, I wonder if I will be able to share some of my own memorial service with my family before I die. Sometimes I wonder why we wait until our days have passed to share our truths and our true feelings with them.

Time will tell and I am sure that the grief box will continue to teach me lessons that I don't always want to learn. Today I added comfort and a feeling of accomplishment for having taken care of my funeral business.

Be brave,

Me

February 7, 2024

Dear Betty,

Last night I was feeling pretty proud of myself. I made a decision and acted on it completely independently. I thought "Don would be proud of me as well." This morning I realized that thinking that he would be proud is more about me wanting him to be proud than something that he would say. This led me to recognize yet another answer to my own question, who am I and where do I go from here?

Lately, I have been told by many, well a few, well maybe a couple, of my friends that I have to let go of control. They remind me that I have ruled the roost, made or at least encouraged many of our life decisions. In so many ways I am happy that Don was not a controlling man. He was more than willing to let me be me, to be in control, manage our home and family. Being told that I have "done" it for so long that I don't have to "do" it anymore. While I agree that I do not want to be a controlling person when it comes to other's lives, being a widow demands some amount of control unless one wants to forget about being independent and become dependent.

So, I ask myself, "What is the difference between being in control and being independent?" For me, it is recognizing what I want to control and what I need to do to maintain my independence. I want to remain independent as an elder-in-training. I have grown through many stages in my life and had amazing mentors along the way. I feel that I have grown into self-sufficiency and for the most part, am self-reliant. I am self-made and I live on my own hump. Self-care and self-identity are the most difficult for me but what I want to maintain now.

Betty, I have decided that it is not all bad to have some control in my life as there are certainly some things that I can't control, and there will probably be more of those as time marches on. I really loved the feeling of independence that I had yesterday and it was because I took control and made a difficult decision.

Don't worry, grief box. I am fully aware that I cannot control your role in my life. I know that grief comes at will. That the very present sense of loss is out of my control. Yet, I wonder, if I could control all of the grief feelings, and could turn them off like a faucet, then would I miss the gifts of this journey? Might I even lose my independence, as well? Can we turn off those parts of our humanness that are too painful? I am sure that is where addiction comes from or the loss of oneself to the complete soul that they are meant to be.

Well, Betty, I am choosing to be controlling. It is what I know how to do. I will be discerning about what I try to control. I hope to maintain my independence and I do not think that I can do it without control.

Grief box, add that to your collection. I choose to be the boss, head held high, calling the shots, running the show, pulling the strings, and ruling the roost. I will also be loving and kind.

Be bold,

Me

February 8, 2024

Dear Betty,

We live on in dreams and memories. Last night I dreamt that I was wandering around a tourist town with little shops. I was looking for help because a large cow had gotten out at the farm. I told Jake that I would go for help. As I came around a corner, standing there with his arms crossed and leaning on a door jam was Don. Boy, Betty, he looked great. Young and handsome. He said, "I was waiting for you." That was it. No more said and I woke up remembering this dream as though I had just lived it. I haven't dreamt about him a lot, but when I do it stays with me, and in some way that I don't understand, it comforts me. I welcome these dreams and hope that they continue to come to me.

Memories are not so easy. At times I try to reach back in time to the best of my memories of Don and even others who have died. Most times this kind of remembering is also comforting, but I must confess that they can also open the grief box and present to me as melancholy and even another bout of tears. I don't want to stop spending time with all of the memories. The happy ones, the puzzling ones, and yes, even the sad ones. They return life to the souls no longer with me. I try not to return to those last days with Don. Then I chide myself because some of my most precious memories were made during that time. The most loving and understanding words spoken.

How am I contributing to the making of the memories that might keep me in mind? It would be so easy at this stage of my life to just let it be. I could step into the background and isolate myself from my loved ones. I could play the martyr but that would not be the authentic me I hope to be. I selfishly want to be remembered and to stay alive in memories and dreams.

Remember me,

Me

February 9, 2024

Dear Betty,

Another empty day. This was my first thought as I awakened this morning. I lay in bed looking up at the ceiling and thinking about what I needed to do today. Nothing, I thought, I really don't have to do anything. No household tasks, no errands to run, no one to hurry to get ready for a doctor's appointment, an empty calendar. There must be an ordinary thing that you can do today, I thought. Of course, there is at least one ordinary thing. Just getting myself out of bed is ordinary, taking the dog out for his morning jaunt is ordinary, getting myself dressed for the day is ordinary. And, thank God, writing to you, Betty, has become ordinary.

After wallowing around in my empty day funk, I found myself. I heard my own voice telling me that there is comfort even in the ordinary. That each day holds as much promise as I am willing to acknowledge. Again, that phrase from the "Desiderata" comes back to niggle at me. "Remember what peace there may be in silence."

Then I remembered another quote from a book I recently read, *"You do not need to know precisely what is happening, or exactly where it is all going. What you need is to recognize the possibilities and challenges offered by the present moment, and to embrace them with courage, faith, and hope." (When Life Speaks Listen,* Linda Piotrowski.)

Thank you, Linda. Listening to life today may just be what I need. "Embracing the ordinary with courage, faith, and hope" I will celebrate the ordinary and fold the laundry with peace in my soul. Maybe tomorrow will be extraordinary!

Here's to you, Betty,

Me

February 11, 2024

Dear Betty,

Unlike two days ago, my first thoughts today were not, 'another empty day.' It is a full day today and it was a full day yesterday. What happened, you might wonder? Well, remember I told you that I visited the funeral home last week and that I felt brave? I offered to do memorial services for families who didn't have a resource, an officiant who could help.

The phone rang and I saw that it was the funeral home calling. My first thought was, "They must need more information." That was not it at all. One of the funeral directors asked if I had offered to officiate a memorial service. "Yes," I replied.

My heart and my soul were suddenly full. How could this be? Now in retrospect, I see that in working so hard to stay faithful to my grief process, I hadn't given much thought to wondering what I might do to move on, to be of service. I hate the phrase "move on" because it immediately makes me feel guilty. I don't ever want to stop remembering or loving or thinking about Don and our life together.

You know, Betty, what he would have said if I could have shared this kind of news with him? He would have said, "Good, honey. You should do that. You are good at it." I will hold on to his imaginary words as I try to hold on to a positive self-image. After all, I still am not sure that I know that old woman who greets me in the mirror each day and my ego still wonders how I will be accepted. No matter, I said yes and I am filled with grace.

Not moving on, making more of my days, feeling full of purpose, and grateful for the reminder to use the gifts we have been given. My sadness is smiling today.

Be full, Betty,

Me

February 13, 2024

Dear Betty,

It is true that when you are engaged in something that you find meaningful, purposeful, things change. Since I started to prepare for the memorial service, I can say that I have felt less empty. I feel content.

As I have been thinking about what I might do next, nothing has seemed to fit the bill. I can think of all sorts of volunteer opportunities but none of them actually made me pick up the phone and do anything about them. My spontaneous offering about memorial services felt right immediately. Of course, Betty, I am a little anxious for all of the reasons I should be. Will they be able to connect with the words that I have written? Will I be able to aid them in their grief or just confuse them even more? How will they accept the way I look? By that Betty, I mean me being an 80-year-old woman and short at that! Aside from that, I am feeling pretty confident in what I have prepared for them.

I am choosing to take appreciation and gratefulness out of the grief box today. I am grateful to the women in my life who grew with me into these skills that I feel so comfortable with. I appreciate the person who has offered me this opportunity.

This indiscernible sadness that has been a part of me these last several months is still there and I really think that it will always be part of me now. Perhaps it will make me better, more compassionate, and more understanding for it.

Onward,

Me

February 14, 2024

Dear Betty,

There is some kind of stomach ailment going around and today I have fallen ill with it. 'Oh no, this can't be happening,' I said to myself. I was just feeling good and purposeful. I have to be well and present for the memorial service on Friday.

I am so glad that I spent most of Monday preparing and feel that at least that is almost ready. Just a bit of fine-tuning. What will happen if I am not well? I guess someone else will just have to deliver it. Not a pleasant thought, depressing even.

I am going to do my best to relax into yet another reality. The world will not end without me.

Sick and sorry for myself,

Me

February 15, 2024

Dear Betty,

Miracles do happen, or it is a fast-moving flu. I am feeling so much better today. I even went to the bank, ran some errands, and am happy to do these ordinary things. I am sure that I will be fine tomorrow.

I talked to one of the family members today and she told me that they do not have anyone who will do a eulogy or even give me a written statement. I feel sad about this. Still, I also understand how hard it is to focus one's thoughts in grief. I could hear the pain in her voice and I hope that I did my best to be affirming and understanding.

Betty, send me good thoughts tomorrow morning. I am going to rest now and I am sure that I will be fit as a fiddle. A deeper sense of compassion is just one of the gifts of my own grief journey. I hope I will learn to use it with my words of celebration of a stranger's life.

Hoping,

Me

February 16, 2024

Dear Betty,

Would I ever have thought that a funeral home would feel comfortable and like a place of belonging? Betty, I met a sad and grieving family. Clearly a family separated by distance and time. Surprised by how many people came to offer their condolences and support, they were grateful.

I felt a sense of belonging. Belonging to the team whose purpose was to bring peace and healing to a bereft family. Again, the word "purpose" comes to me now but at the time I was just happy and honored that I had something to give. It felt like the skills that I have acquired through the years and the process of traveling my own grief journey allowed me to be present in the moment to let them touch my own heart and I hope, Betty, that I was able to touch theirs as well.

How is it that entering into someone else's pain or experience openly and honestly turns into a gift for myself? I have no answers. Something has changed inside me, there is a crack in my sadness. I feel ready to be open to where the road takes me. What kind of light will fill the crack?

Wondering,

Me

February 18, 2024

Dear Betty,

This morning I was listening to a book by Sue Monk Kidd. This chapter was about letting go. I have wrestled with the letting go concept in grief. Each time it comes up I throw up my hands and wish I had a red stop sign. Stop already. What is it that causes such a strong reaction in me?

Letting go is just too final. Yes, I know that there are times in our lives when we need to let go of something completely. For me, grief is not one of them. It is more like I am on this journey; I have committed to the journey. I am traveling down a road through an undeveloped countryside. There are no road signs to tell me how far it is to the next stop. Or if there even is a next stop. Finally, after passing through the burgs of feelings I meet a fellow traveler who tells me that I have to let go. Don't look behind, only be in the present, and don't worry about the future.

Here is where I throw up my stop sign. I rebel at leaving go of all that the past has given me. I rebel at the idea of letting go of my loving memories. I rebel at letting go, leaving behind the lessons learned and the feelings I have experienced in my grief box.

Does letting go have to mean forgetting, tough-
ening up, moving on? Is letting go really making
room for something new? Why can't then and now
co-exist? Letting go is like dropping a coin into a
cavern and not hearing it fall.

Is letting go like not holding on? If I let go of all
that I am or all that I love or all that I have come to
be, who am I? I will continue on my grief journey
because I cannot. My bags are not too heavy and
I know that the future road sign will soon appear.
I will hold on to all that is for me and wait for the
crack in my grief to break fully open making room
for tomorrow's light.

Holding on, Betty,

Me

February 19, 2024

Dear Betty,

What a day! The phone has not stopped ringing. How am I feeling today? I am trying to find the words to describe how I feel. There is the all-the-time sad that I have told you about several times. Beyond that, I am remembering how supported I felt when I could talk to Don about something that I did, like officiating a memorial service. I really miss asking him about an issue that I am trying to work through and having him share his perspective. He was really good at helping me work through thoughts and feelings.

So, I guess I feel a little lost today. Feeling like I need to find new ways to process some things while trying to hold on to listening to his voice, at least the one that I imagine I am hearing. So many things that I realize I have had the good fortune to have in my partner, my friend, my spouse, and my love. I miss them all.

Betty, thank you again for being with me on this journey.

Teary,

Me

February 21, 2024

Dear Betty,

What is the difference between being alone and being a-lone? Being a loner has never been a problem for me, well, maybe once in a while. Like when I didn't feel like I belonged to a certain group or in the midst of a conversation that I just couldn't relate to. I am alone now. I do not have a partner, a roommate, someone that I have to care for, except York, of course.

This morning I went to do my ordinary thing. I went to the grocery store. While I was driving through the countryside, I was trying to put a name to what I am feeling today. I thought I am a-lone. No one with me to talk to or complain to about the price of groceries or the state of politics in our country today. I have to continue to get comfortable about doing things as a loner. No arm to link mine into, no one to open the door for me, no one to help put the groceries away.

So today I am feeling sorry. Sorry that I no longer have these things and wishing that I would have appreciated them when I had them. Don't get me wrong, Betty, I did appreciate those things because Don was really good at them. I just think that there is a different kind of appreciation when it comes through grief. Can't go back, don't feel especially regretful about it, just want to accept that once again, something that I took for granted is greatly missed. I am sorry for not always being present to what is right in front of my eyes.

Appreciate you, Betty,

Me

February 22, 2024

Dear Betty,

Can one be a little depressed? Is there a scale that measures the level of depression? I am sure that there is. This morning I was busy mixing the dough for the bread I am making later today. I started to think about my daily question. "What am I feeling today?" My answer: quiet and a little depressed. Then I thought, 'Oh no, you better not say that, better find another way to say how you are feeling.' Checking in with Merriam-Webster was for the first time not helpful. There were two words that seemed to make sense. "Feeling low." Yep, that is me today. Not pushed down or flattened like a pancake; just not at the top of my game.

Why is it do you think that we think we have to be so guarded about what we say? If I told the family that I felt a little depressed, I am sure that they would have me signed up for an appointment at the counseling clinic before I could say "jackrabbit." So, do you think that if I say I am just feeling a little low, they will try to cheer me up? What funny creatures we are.

I went to a meeting of a small group of like-minded folks last night. We have been meeting for some time now. We are all about the same age and experience and our common bond has been the community theater. We just learned that one of our members died. He was such an important voice in the group. Oddly, we didn't talk about him. Too close to the bone for now, I think. I am sure there will be many conversations about him and what he meant to the group when we are further along in our joint grief journey.

Well, Betty, I think I will get on with my ordinary day and stuff a little depression into the grief box. Was sure something to ponder though.

Feeling low,

Me

February 26, 2024

Dear Betty,

It is over. The rehearsal, rehearsal dinner, and the wedding of my grandson Nikolaus and his wife Tabitha. All went well and today I am thinking about what comes next.

It was of course a bit melancholy because Don was not with us. I miss dancing with him and the wonderful way he had of being with his family. Always remembering to dance with each of his girls.

One of the things that I miss most is having him here to talk about things that I am doing or things that I am thinking about doing. I am not sure that I always wanted his opinion but I sure would like to have it now.

Feeling pleased today. Glad that everything went well for the bride and groom. It is always delightful to watch the young couples enjoying themselves. Still, each of them remarked that they were missing him as well.

Till tomorrow,

Me

February 27, 2024

Dear Betty,

Two days after the wedding, I am still tired and realizing that my aging legs rebel when expected to dance like a teenager. Aside from that I am once again confronted with the fact that this grief journey is far from over. Just when I think that I have gotten my equilibrium back in tow, *wham!* Foggy brain, heartsick, and wondering why I continue to fight it all. Let it go, echoes through me and reminds me how often I have said those very words to someone else. Still, I tell myself that I promised myself that I would not just "let it go" but rather stay in the process, come what may. I may regret this at some time. For now, I am still embracing the journey and finding new degrees of sadness right along new degrees of hope.

I have managed the holidays and even my birthday with some aplomb. Not so much the wedding weekend. Don would have been in his Papa role and loving every minute. I would have been talking his ear off as I tried to process the event. He would have listened and offered his quiet observations and I would have replied with at least some, "Oh sure. Easy for you to say." By now, Betty, you are hearing my missing in this missive.

What next? Who knows? All is quiet around here today. Some of the families have returned home, others back to work, and life just keeps rolling along.

Wondering,

Me

February 28, 2024

Dear Betty,

It always seems that the day or two after an event makes me feel like I haven't made any progress on my grief journey road. I know that this isn't true, but it does feel that way some days. I try to reason it out and then I think, "What am I doing?" There is no reason or understanding. I thought that I was pretty emotionally healthy. I even did a session once on emotional maturity. It is not that I have never heard of some of the emotions that I have been wrestling with, but it is new territory for me now because it is so focused.

Today's weather is a great metaphor for my emotional wellness. Yesterday it was 70 degrees and sunny. I was outside and enjoying the warmth wearing jeans and a cotton shirt. This morning I stepped out of bed to find that the temperature had dropped 40 degrees. Yesterday the wind was calm and quiet and today it is ripping around with gusts at almost 50 miles an hour.

Yep, Betty, one day I am calm and quiet and the next my emotions are tearing through me with no rhyme or reason.

Today I try to practice again the lesson of the "Desiderata", "Remember what peace there may be in silence."

OK, Betty, I did say TRY. My silence today feels like woebegone.

Be still my soul,

Me

February 29, 2024

Dear Betty,

Familiar phrases can at times be as wonderful and as painful as memories. Today I was remembering how Don would come home from wherever and he would say, "Hello, the house." Or "Hi honey, I'm home." Whenever anyone left our house after a visit he would always say, "Be safe and enjoy your day." It was also his way of saying thank you to customers at the farm market. I don't know what made me think about these except I guess I was simply missing hearing these familiar phrases.

Betty, remember when I wrote about memories being wonderful and fickle? That is why I am putting familiar phases in the same category. Yes, I get teary in these memory moments and still I don't want to lose the sound of his voice in my mind and heart.

Listening,

Me

MARCH

March 1, 2024

Dear Betty,

Today I learned that a young friend of mine lost his young father. I am so sorry for them. It was a long illness and everyone knew that it was coming but one cannot prepare for the finality of death. I am weeping for them today and if, I am honest, I am weeping for myself too.

My emotions are flowing like a river going over a dam. Rushing, rushing, tumbling into the deep water below, catching my breath, and then hoping for someone or something to jolt me back onto safe ground. If I thought that I understood empathy before I am certain that I have a far better grasp of it now. I ache for the pain that they are feeling now.

Betty, all of this reminds me of a conversation that I had with a friend yesterday. This friend is my age or close to it. I was trying to share with her some of the truth of my grief journey. I asked her if she would like to read some of my letters to you. She said no, she thought that they were too personal. I get that. However, I find that it is really hard for others to understand mine or anyone else's grief. Until I started the journey into my own, I don't think that I was very empathetic either.

When we just want someone, anyone, just to listen, or when we are starving for any kind of understanding by way of sharing our journey, it is hurtful for another person to reject an invitation into our journey.

You are the best,

Me

March 2, 2024

Dear Betty,

Another page has turned on the calendar. Hard to believe that I have been traveling this journey for six months already. Some days it seems like yesterday. I find myself still in the throes of those last days. The feelings around the memories have softened and when I remember some of our conversations I can even smile.

Ordinary days. Folded the laundry, washed a kettle left too long to soak, wrote out bills, went out and played with the dog and there is still much of the day left. I am thankful for the lesson of ordinary things because they help to chase away the doldrums, they give me purpose.

Betty, do you think that ordinary days and ordinary things might just be another way to escape the longing for a clear road map for this journey? Sometimes I feel that way. Thankfully those feelings don't last too long and I remember to be grateful for the kindness of the man who shared the lesson with me when he was traveling on his own grief journey.

"You are unique." How many times did we share this simple phrase with the countless women who gathered in our circles? Never have I felt the truth of this statement as I do now. "There is no one on the planet exactly like you," we said. It is true that there may be others with similar looks, beliefs, or experiences, but deep down in the emotional part of our being, we are unique. When unique grief came knocking on my door, I came to understand its challenge and its gift. There is not a person on this planet who can completely identify with my journey nor I theirs. We can try to have empathy and compassion. Two more words added to the grief box that I have come to feel in ways humbling, deep, and like never before.

Betty, unique grief feels lonely in a comfortable way. "Remember what peace there may be in silence." (Max Ehrmann)

Alone,

Me

March 3, 2024

Dear Betty,

"No one will entirely understand what it is like to live with our specific shattering. There is something beautiful about this. Our particular grief reflects the particular wonder of what we had—a grace that visited our life in a way designed especially for us. Yet this very quality can compound our grief because it leaves us feeling so alone. One of grief's most insidious aspects lies in how isolating it can become. This aspect of grief calls for intentionality from us: that we resist grief's capacity to cut us off from those around us at the time we need them most." (Jan Richardson)

As serendipity would have it, I found this quote at precisely the time I had been thinking about feeling isolated. I agree that grief is a specialist. No matter how empathetic family or friends are, only I can own my grief. It is hard to embrace the idea that there is something beautiful about this. It does not feel beautiful like a graced moment. Yes, there are moments of feeling that what we had was amazing and ours alone. In the pain of its loss, it is difficult to be okay with the isolation.

How many kinds of isolation are there? Many I guess, self-isolation, cultural isolation, emotional isolation, and more. The isolation that I am feeling now is particular to my grief and the journey it has set me to. It becomes clear to me now after these months of travel that even when another person has also taken this journey their story is not my story. In this I agree with the Jan Richardson quote. Just when our hearts are longing for understanding, agreement, and empathy, we realize that it cannot be. There is compassion and caring, so much kindness but clearly the grief journey and the grief isolation is one that only the self can either face, give voice to, and in some way try to embrace.

When lately I have tried to share bits and pieces of my journey, I understand that although the person I am offering my authentic self to wants to understand, they simply cannot because it is my loss, personal and isolating. Perhaps we humans just don't like hearing sad stories? Unlike some of the other kinds of isolation, it is not self-inflicted or other inflicted either. I wonder if it is just another bit of wisdom gleaned on the grief journey that I have determined to take.

Learning,

Me

March 5, 2024

Dear Betty,

I am in the office looking at my large prayer plant. The sun is shining on some of the leaves making them transparent and a really pretty light yellow. The leaves underneath and away from the sun are dark, dark green with lighter-colored veins. The sun has found a pocket through it and has given light to one corner of a dark leaf. Some of their leaves are curled up in prayer.

Yet another metaphor appears. If I were the plant, I would be enjoying the warmth of the upper leaves. Hints of transparency. I find hope there even though there is still plenty of dark below to still be explored. The veins are showing me that there are many options connecting me to the main vein. In the end, so many prayers curled up and reaching for the sun.

Thank you, prayer plant.

Praying,

Me

March 6, 2024

Dear Betty,

Today I will admit that my heart is aching. It seems that I am once again on the downside of the roller coaster ride. Too many days of sad news. Too many wishes for some good news. This of course is confessing that I don't want to hear about how some of the sad news is good news. How can that be?

For some the phrase, "they are not suffering anymore," or "they are in a better place" is perhaps good news. I don't think that I will ever feel that the loss of any of those who have touched my life, who I have loved dearly, is good news.

Yes, Betty, I realize that these sentiments are meant to aid in my grief. They are offered with all good intentions. It is on me to decide how I will accept them.

Spring, it seems, is knocking on our door earlier than usual. The lilac bush is budding, the grass is turning green and there have been many days of blue skies and sunshine. Does this make me feel any less lonely or sad? Maybe a bit. It also makes me face my sense of loss again. No early spring ride in the countryside and no one sharing plans for what to plant in the garden this year. No one here.

I am going out to lunch with a dear friend today. She listens, she hears, and she shares. She is the best of the best kind of friend a person on the grief journey could hope for. She is kinda like you, Betty.

Reaching out,

Me

March 8, 2024

Dear Betty,

It is a rainy, dreary day. Good day to try to declutter my office. Maybe I should think about decluttering my emotions. They seem to be rather cluttered these past few days. A few days ago, I said that I was once again on the roller coaster of grief emotions. I said that I was once again at the bottom. Today I can say that I have begun the climb back up. I don't know why I have chosen the roller coaster as a metaphor; I don't even like them. Still, in my imagination, I can sense the drastic ups and downs. That alone might be why I think it works.

When do we discover if we are the kind of person who likes to live alone or one who likes to live with another person? I never gave it much thought. I had made my choice so many years ago that it just didn't cross my mind. It has been pretty quiet around here the last several days. At times I felt lonely. At other times I miss having another person to watch TV with or just to talk to. And I even wished that I could ask, "What should we have for dinner tonight?" even when it meant the answer was, "Whatever." My conclusion is that I did enjoy being married. I did like living with another person.

Betty, I am not sure that I am fully content with living alone but for now it is OK. Actually, I think it is good and it is also okay to admit that at times it is not so good.

I prepared tonight's dinner this morning so I don't have to worry about that later. I plan on taking advantage of this rainy, dreary day to curl up in my favorite chair with my cozy blanket and watch a movie. It might be a good one or a thought-provoking one. Who knows? Will I miss the company or, methinks, I might just enjoy the solitary experience?

Both/And,

Me

March 9, 2024

Dear Betty,

Tears running down my face, tired of doing and thinking about ordinary things. Grief box is dusty because I don't want to look inside, exhausted, not willing to feel or name my emotional state today.

Too many days empty and alone, disliking weekends.

Sorry Betty, that will do it for poor me today. Seems I took a detour off the grief journey road. Back to the road map tomorrow.

Still traveling,

Me

March 10, 2024

Dear Betty,

It seems, Betty, that the grief box has a mind of its own. Not only did I find it open yesterday but also found myself back to square one. You know like when you are playing with a game board and someone gets a turn and lands on your piece. Then they can send you back to the beginning. That's how I felt yesterday. I was never much good at board games but certainly remember what it was like to have to start over.

Every little thing that happened yesterday sent me not only teary, but sobbing. Memories from long ago that I hadn't visited in years. I had been feeling lonely and left out. Then, one by one people started showing up. A grandson came to play with York. My great-granddaughter appeared with her parents and, finally, my daughter came through the door. I thought that my silent woes must have been heard and the universe sent out the message. I think it was grace.

Last evening, I watched the movie *Out of Africa.*"It was one of Don's favorites. As I watched the movie, I wondered why he liked it so much. I saw it differently while I was trying to see it through his eyes. Watching in this way was revealing in such good ways. I think it really helped me know him in ways that I probably knew before but couldn't articulate as clearly. The more I watched through tears of sadness and love, the deeper the understanding that came to me.

All in all, today I am telling you, Betty, it was an extraordinary day. I know that I have mentioned these days before. I felt the pain of grief so deeply. More deeply than even before. Still the grace of understanding let me rest last night in a new kind of awareness and peace.

As time continues to separate the now from the then of Don's death, I wonder what other memories might surface that will cause me such deep grief. What other memories will come calling that bring me yet a deeper understanding of our lives then and mine now.

We began daylight savings time today. We took a leap forward hopefully into spring. Will I be able to leap forward into a new season of my feeling self or will I, just like the clock, fall back? Perhaps the gift is the knowing that it is all part of the process. Give and take. Forward and back. All the while letting time separate the now from the then and the reality of his death.

Me

March 12, 2024

Dear Betty,

Yesterday I named my feelings as sad, down, lost, and poor me. Today I told myself to get my shit together and tried to block out all of the lessons I have learned so far on this journey. I wanted to throw out the grief box and, clearly, I didn't write to you either.

Now I feel like a naughty child who just had to have a temper tantrum. You know what Betty? It actually felt good. I cried, ranted, carried on, and hoped that no one would show up for a visit. My friend Dre tells me all of the time that I have always been the one in control. I have been the one taking care of things and so now I shouldn't be surprised that I do not have any—I mean any—control other than what I think would put me into denial. Do you see that it is a complete contradiction to everything that I have been telling you these past months?

I will tell you that I am a spiritual person. Not a religious one. There have been times in my life when being a religious one was helpful and needed to get me to where I am today. I received grace today, or a blessing, if you prefer. I have a book of daily readings that I got from my daughter. Today's message was about trust and hope. It offered the chance to let someone else show you the path forward. 'Great,' I thought, 'just what I need.' I mean that in the best way. Then, I decided to check Face-book. I do not do that regularly but today there was a post from one of my cousins. We grew up together and she is definingly a religious and a spiritual woman. Her post started out by saying, "Trust with all of your heart and do not lean on your own understanding. Acknowledge Him and He will make your paths straight."

So, Betty, do with that what you will, but I am going to try my best to trust and hope and seek out the path offered.

Blessed,

Me

March 13, 2024

Dear Betty,

I was watching a TV show. It was one of the oldies but goodies. It was, however, one of the sad episodes. I found myself tearing up and that brought me to my question for today. Are ordinary tears different than grief tears? Yes, of course they are, I said to myself. Ordinary tears are those that just happen because something strikes you in your human compassionate place.

Grief tears are brought on because you are open to your many grief feelings. Sometimes they are a trickle down the cheeks as you remember something fond, a time that you know will not ever be the same again. Other times they are pouring down in buckets. I find that these tears are reserved for the unexpected times that creep up on me when I least expect them. Mostly when I am ever so sad, lost, lonely, or undone, believing that I will never be my old self again. I am not even sure what I mean "my old self" to be.

Today I read, "Don't get caught up in your circumstances." 'Easier said than done,' I thought. Still Betty, I hope that I am learning and responding to my circumstances rather than getting caught up in them. When I get caught up, I spiral into poor-me syndrome and I have resolved not to stay there.

Well, not for long anyway, Betty.

Back on track?

Me

March 14, 2024

Dear Betty,

The other day I said that I was feeling lost. Now I am wondering just what that means. What was I trying to say and what does "lost" feel like for me?

It is not like I was on a path and just lost my way. I have pretty consistently been on the same grief journey, many road signs (feelings) but the same path. It is not like I have been about something and got lost in it or thought that it was a misstep.

I guess that I am not lost after all if I choose to use my own definition of lost. What am I? Weary of finding myself on the same long road to me. Ah ha! Maybe it is about self-identity. I am certain that I am not the same woman I was just a few months ago. I do not have the same role to play, or the same masks to wear. I do still have the same values and yes, the same gifts to share. I just don't seem to have a map to that location. I love and care and learn and wait.

Waiting has never been one of my strong suits. I don't wait well. Don would agree and has in the past. Yes, Betty, I have thought of many things that I could do, volunteer for, join. But something in me says, 'Not yet, grief is not finished with you.' Will it ever be finished with me? I think not. I do think that grief and I will find a way to live with one another and together we will continue to fill the grief box. Even in the doing of ordinary things.

As much as I struggle with it, silence can bring the gift of peace. Some days, though, I would like to rebel and jump into the noise and haste, whatever that may be.

Good day,

Me

March 15, 2024

Dear Betty,

Today I like ordinary things. Today I know what I have to do. I am going to the bank, I am going to vacuum, and I am going to take York out for his walk. There, now, I have a plan. Ordinally things are distractions and who says that a little distraction isn't a good thing once in a while?

Staying present to my grief journey is my choice. I have been told that I don't have to stay focused, that I can make other choices whenever I want. Yes, Betty, this is true. But! As my friend Dre tells me all of the time, "You have always been in control, taking care of everything, solving all of the problems." I usually bristle when she tells me this. You know, it is my choice and I have made it. At the end of this journey, I believe that I will be a better me.

This journey will never be totally over. There are lessons learned and more to come. I am sure that I will return to the memories of this time many times. And being a person who wants to experience all of it and a person who feels a need to finish something once she is committed to it, I will keep on traveling. Some days now I almost feel my shine coming back.

What am I feeling today? Teetering, positive like Pooh, and missing him.

Keep moving,

Me

March 16, 2024

Dear Betty,

Today we celebrated two birthdays: Caryn, my oldest daughter, and Roger, my son-in-law. It was a nice event and they were both surprised. I once again felt like an observer but in a good way. It is interesting to notice the interactions of all of the generations. I am coming to believe that Don was a bigger force to be reckoned with than I ever thought him to be.

What I really want to share with you today, Betty, is something that happened toward the end of the party. A few of us were sitting at a table visiting and waiting while others were saying their goodbyes. I was sitting. One of my grandsons came over and was standing next to me. Without even noticing what I was doing I slipped my hand into his. He didn't react at all, just stood there holding my hand.

Later last night, while rehearsing the events of the day, I remembered the incident. I would have thought that it would have sent me to tears but it did not. It felt nice. It was a fond remembering of something that Don and I would do often. Just a little bit of "I know you are here and I am here with you."

No tears this time, just the grace of another's presence. So many little things.

Holding hands,

Me

March 17, 2024

Dear Betty,

Today I am happy that I am not Irish. People used to think that I was because of my name. I truly am not. If I were and if we had always celebrated it, I think that it would just be another excuse for sadness. Instead, I have something else to share with you.

Recently I came across a book by C.S. Lewis titled *A Grief Observed.* It is a small book but bigger than life to me these past few days. He is sharing his journal about the death of his wife. The foreword by Madeleine L'Engle also touched my heart and soul.

I thought, 'Who am I to think that my experience is anything like theirs?' Yet, why not me? Of all of the things that I have read and searched through for some understanding of my grief journey, this little book has come the closest. It is like coming home to someone who shares what others cannot comprehend. I don't think it is because they don't want to, but rather, they just have to travel their own unique and pebble-strewn road. It doesn't matter where the understanding comes from, just that it does. So, Betty, today I am grateful for C.S. Lewis and Madeleine L'Engle.

I will share more about this experience as I continue to absorb all that it has offered to me. I think that I will read and listen to this grace many times.

A graced moment,

Me

March 18, 2024

Dear Betty,

I was a little let down today after the party yesterday. These days I am happy for the getaway moments that seem to come just when I need them.

As I heard yesterday from most of the families, they were off to celebrate St. Pat's Day. Now, Betty, I don't want you to think that I am telling you this because I am feeling maudlin. No, I just want to share another awareness. I was alone and quiet. It occurred to me that I am now a family of one. Oh sure, I still have my big and beautiful family, but they are all grown and growing their own "families" and making new memories. At times I am invited to join them as I did yesterday. Other times they are making family memories on their own. This is how it should be. I remember well the times I was happy that for some holiday or other plans changed and we found ourselves celebrating with just our own "family."

I am now my own family. I do have my faithful dog and my crazy cat and I suppose in a way they are my family.

Truthfully, at first, I felt a little left out but then I did feel good about being OK with being one with myself. Grief box sitting firmly on itself.

I smiled while I remembered Don singing "Danny Boy." No, we are not Irish and it was just a little out of his reach but we enjoyed it anyway.

Happy Patty's Day

Me

March 19, 2024

Dear Betty,

I woke up this morning feeling quite bright and shiny. I very boldly and confidently decided that I was going to put a lid on the grief box. As I thought about doing just that, I started to think about all of the things that had fallen out of the grief box. I thought about all of the things that I have put into the grief box. Now I am not so sure that I am ready to put the lid on it after all.

Betty, do you think that this is the beginning of my being ready to travel on to the next crossroads in this journey? For that little while, for a little blip in time, I felt lighter, happy even. Then I got real. I am fully aware that each day is just a little different than the last; the grief box may crack open evermore. I do find myself recalling really significant, challenging, and lovely times in our relationship. I do not find myself as quickly reliving the last days.

Still Betty, something has shifted, I am not sure that I would say this is acceptance. We have had that discussion before. Another awareness, maybe, but really it is more about how I feel than what I think.

I guess that this means that you will continue to hear from me.

Changing,

Me

March 23, 2024

Dear Betty,

Two days ago, I met with the Kindreds. The whole time was filled with new awareness for me. Each of them is dealing with issues related to aging and relationships. As I listened and tried to facilitate the information about the issue at hand, it became so clear to me that I would not ever relate to some of what they were sharing in the same way again.

My grief journey it seems has opened a new window of understanding. I was engaged in their stories but at the same time felt somehow disconnected. It is true that I have confronted some of the same issues that they are wrestling with now. As I listened, the issues that were so confounding to them seemed clear to me. I am not sure how my current journey has changed my perspective, but I know that it has in meaningful ways.

When all of the "grief experts" talk about isolation, they most often posit that the person in grief self-isolates. Grief is so different for each of us that I believe for some, self-isolation is needed for their own healing. I am not experiencing that. I don't even know if isolation is the right word for what I am sensing in myself. I do know that in the Kindred conversation, I felt removed and isolated, thinking that sharing my thoughts was not appropriate or helpful to them. I think that I am seeing through a different lens, one that has become clear on some matters. I am at peace with being where I am and letting them be where they are. Still, I feel a real belonging.

This doesn't mean that I was not engaged or present to the conversation. I did offer my thoughts and feelings at times. I felt a little like I was missing the mark or speaking just a little off-center. I have never been one to tell you what you want to hear and still I am not at all sure that there is understanding from them. This is not a fault. It is just coming from a very different place of separating the ribbons of grief feelings.

Looking in,

Me

March 25, 2024

Dear Betty,

It seems that I am not writing to you as frequently. I am involved in my new adventure of officiating memorial services. Maybe I am more engaged in my head than in my many feelings.

I am not deceiving myself into believing that I am done with the grief box. Perhaps it will just not show itself as regularly.

I have to remember that there are positive feelings in the box. All was not negative or sad.

Wondering,

Me

March 28, 2024

Dear Betty,

Remember what peace there may be in silence. These words have been floating around in my head like colorful balloons just waiting for me to puncture them.

In the early days of grief, I railed at them. "There is no peace," I said. "How can I be at peace? What is there to be peaceful about?"

Now, several months later, I am sure that the peace has to do with purpose. Finding your purpose and deciding who you want to be when you grow up are familiar phrases in today's pop culture. People in the last chapter of their lives are still asking the same questions as their grandchildren and great-grandchildren.

I scoffed at the same questions. In grief, it seemed that I had lost all purpose and identity. For most of my life, I knew who I was and what I was doing. I was a mother, wife, grandmother and now a great-grandmother, even a friend. Each of those titles presumes purpose. What does a mother do, what does a wife do, etc.? Now I am popping one balloon at a time and discovering what it is a widow does.

These days I am grateful and at ease with what each day brings by way of the silence. I am sure that there is more to experience and to mourn, but for today, I embrace the silence and I do feel grateful and at ease.

Listening,

Me

March 31, 2024

Dear Betty,

I am sad and weepy today. Not sure why but it is Easter and I miss him asking me what I am baking and what we are doing today. He knows full well but he always asks. I think it was part of our ritual.

I officiated a memorial service two days ago. Maybe I am just now processing and letting myself relax from the adrenaline of the preparation and the event. I am so grateful that they continue to ask me to help with these services. It is something that I enjoy and that I have certainly been preparing for my whole life. It is filling the space of needing to have purpose and to be of service to another.

Yesterday I did something completely out of character for me. I went to the local jewelry shop. Don had a class ring and I had my sister's. I asked the jeweler if he could make me a ring from the two of them. He was so kind and asked me great questions. He wanted to know what I wanted to do with the ring and if it had purpose. After more conversation and looking at some of the ready-made rings that he had, we agreed on a design. I am buying myself a memorial ring. Sometimes I feel like I am losing my mind, or at least my stability. I am, at my whole new ministry and making choices for myself that I didn't think I could make. But, yep, Betty,

I am spending the money and buying something just for me.

Well, Betty, need to go, celebrating Easter with the family. It will be a good day.

Trusting,

Me

APRIL

April 1, 2024

Dear Betty,

Turning another page on the calendar, hard to believe that it has been seven months. Still some days it feels like a lifetime.

I found myself feeling very sad and weepy yesterday. Then this morning the lyrics to a Miley Cyrus song "Wrecking Ball" came to mind. This is what it feels like. A wrecking ball of grief, and that is how it is these days. There is no more slowly falling into it. There, it seems, are not the same feelings that are just there and quietly consuming me. I go along feeling some of the old energy and purpose and then without warning, bam … there it is.

I don't feel as though it takes as long to put the pieces back together as it did just a short time ago. Nonetheless, it is not something that I hope will linger. I want to stuff it back into the grief box if in fact it came from there. If not, I do not want to give it any of my focus.

Once again, I hear my inner voice saying just experience it and let it go.

Trying out my smile,

Me

April 2, 2024

Dear Betty,

It occurs to me that I write to you more about the weather on dreary/wet/rainy days than on sunny ones. Today is one of those days. I could write a lot about this particular metaphor. I am sure you know what that would sound like. I am feeling a bit dreary again today. It is cold with constant rain. Nothing exciting about it, just the kind of day that makes me feel like I don't want to go anywhere or do much of anything.

I see that the grass is turning green. Can I find hope in this rainy metaphor that seems to appear so often? I want to, I really do. Somedays I can touch into the more positive feelings in the g box. Hopeful feelings, grateful feelings, maybe I will soon be able to say like Judy Garland, "Tomorrow, tomorrow, I love ya tomorrow." Is tomorrow really only a day away and another mile gone on this journey?

The grass is turning green, the lilac bush is budding, the daffodils have come to call, and it is, after all, the season of resurrection.

I am missing the absent one, I am sad, I am recognizing the gift of spring, and I know that she is singing for me.

Hope and wonder are just around the corner.

Waiting,

Me

April 3, 2024

Dear Betty,

After all of my positive words of yesterday, Betty, I am confessing to you today that I sobbed all afternoon yesterday. I was cursing this grief journey. The hell with the grief box. Then I found myself once again talking myself off of the ledge of loneliness and a tiny bit of depression and came around to acknowledging that the grief box does hold positive feelings as well.

Do you know the child's toy that is a spinning top? Not the one where you push down the handle but the one that looks like a tool used for darning. It is circular with a point on the end that holds it up to spin. Sometimes it has a string on the top pulled to make it spin. It was my metaphor yesterday. I felt like a spinning top. All my emotions were spinning around but standing in the center while all of the world was racing around me. I felt lonely and out of control.

Betty, I wonder if I would have these insights if I had not decided to face this grief journey openly. I wonder if I would not have the moments of aloneness and silence that have given me a new sense of being. I am not spinning today. Today I am grateful for the grief box and ordinary things, I am grateful for the gift of remembrance, the good memories and the sad ones. I am grateful for you, Betty. You help me work things out honestly, painfully and joyfully.

Till then,

Me

A Hundred Black Birds

A hundred black birds feasting on my grass,

No, feasting on the worms found in my grass

after the long-awaited rain last night.

They must have put out a call

to all the neighbors to come

feast with us there is plenty for all

What do I find to feast on after the rain?

Can I find it in me to share the feast with another,
with my neighbors?

It seems to me that whether the sun shines now
after the rain or not

the feast remains and I think must be shared.

Mary Bub

GLOSSARY

Bethany – The name of a women's organization dedicated to helping women find their authentic voice.

Bird Apartments – The three big evergreen trees in the front yard that house the nests of small birds.

Circle Basics – The agreement made between the participants of a Gathering Circle. Confidentiality, Reflective Listening, Sharing of stories, Ownership, Taking responsibility for one's own needs. Commitment to the shared intent.

Gathering Circle – A safe container in which stories can be shared without judgement. It is a process with a clear intent.

Grief Box – An imaginary place in one's mind used to store emotions.

Kindreds – A Gathering Circle of women coming together to share their thoughts and feelings about specific issues pertinent to them and agreed upon by all members of the circle.

WRWI – Wisconsin Rural Women's Initiative – A private non-profit organization whose mission it is to empower women living primarily in rural areas. The ultimate goal is to effect systemic change within families and their communities through the unique Gathering Circle process. WRWI promotes wellness by developing personal skills and cultivates transformation in a safe environment.

Note: The dictionary quotes throughout the book are from *Merriam-Webster.*

ACKNOWLEDGMENTS

Here I want to acknowledge and offer my gratitude.

For Daniel Lockwood and the staff of the Haase Lockwood Funeral Home for their professionalism, care and compassion.

For Dr. Ronald Hull for teaching me the importance of doing ordinary things.

For Lis Friemuth—the friend I don't want to share. She gives me permission to be Me.

For Linda Piotrowski who graced me with the title of this book. She told me that I should publish the letters and she was side by side with me through the whole process.

For Pat Chaloux who read the first draft of the Letters and who affirmed me by sharing how they had impacted her life.

For Joan, Rita, Mary, Peg, Diane—the Kindreds. They believed in me.

For Christy Harteau, my middle daughter who became my editor, mentor and companion always telling me to just keep writing because I had words.

For Roger Harteau, my son-in-law whose shoulders we stand on. He is my rock and my shield.

For my children and grandchildren, and all of the fine in-laws who I claim as mine as well. They seem to get excited about anything that I take on. I am their Nana.

For Dre. Although she is gone now, I still hear the echo of her voice telling me to stay the course. She was a friend and mentor and I miss her every day.

For the many women who have graced my life with their trust, wisdom and encouragement, and their love.

For Don. He always, always supported my endeavors. The good ones, the silly ones and the ones that didn't always work out. He was there and always on my mind. He wanted me to write a book.

For Elizabeth Hill and her colleagues at Green Heart Living Press. Their patience with this first-time author and their encouragement and expertise made me feel like an old pro.

About the Author

Mary Bub is a grassroots activist, social innovator, author, artist, and photographer. She is the co-founder, past president, and currently an advisor of Wisconsin Rural Women's Initiative, a non-profit organization that provides on-site grassroots programs to individual women and organizations through a Gathering Circle process promoting personal development, transformation, and systemic change. She is the winner of the Social Innovation Prize in Wisconsin for 2008, A Purpose Prize Fellow with Civic Ventures, a recipient of the Feminarian Award, and a winner of Wisconsin's Top Rural Development Initiatives. In addition to *Letters to Betty*, Mary is the author of *A Woman in My Soul, The Angel of the Wood,* and *This is No Merry Widow's Story.*

Mary is a widow, mother, grandmother, great-grandmother, friend, facilitator of a small circle of Kindreds, and Officiant of Memorial Services. She lives on MoonStar Farm with her dog York and cat Liza.

www.marybubauthor.com

www.ingramcontent.com/pod-product-compliance
Lightning Source LLC
Chambersburg PA
CBHW061726120626
46550CB00005B/1718